SURVIVAL GAMES

The Specter of American Debticide

ISBN-13: 978-0692948477 (Custom Universal)
ISBN-10: 0692948473

Library of Congress Control Number: 2017915602

Published by Kindinger Strategic Advisors, LLC
3130 Indian Trail
Eustis, Florida 32726

Cover design by Streetlight Graphics

DEDICATION

To Cindy whose patience and support made this project possible.

TABLE OF CONTENTS

Survival Games

TABLE OF EXHIBITS

Part I - Revisiting Mega Fatality Risk

Introduction

I am compelled to introduce this book with an apology. *Survival Games* is not an easy read that follows a simple narrative through a pleasant journey to a satisfying conclusion. It is the record of an investigation (these are currently popular) that begins with a modest attempt to demonstrate the power of quantitative risk analysis and leads through history and scientific inquiry to current day economics and politics. The conclusions it reaches about the collective risks we face are disturbing, but I hope they might inspire us all to be sure that we win the survival games.

Chapter 1 The Origins of Mega Fatality Risk

Section IV of my first book *Risk Management Revisited (RMR)* presented a quantitative risk analysis demonstrating the risk assessment principles and methods introduced in the earlier parts of the book.   The subject I selected for this demonstration analysis was existential risk, or hazards that could threaten the existence of the human race. The name I gave to this effort is the *Mega Fatality Risk Assessment* (MFRA). I thought this would be a subject of interest to most everyone and, when I could not find any previous attempt to assemble an integrated quantitative estimate of mega fatality risk, I thought I might even produce something useful. The task was fun to do and the results at least somewhat surprising.

To fully appreciate this book it is important to understand not only the results of the MFRA but also the risk assessment concepts, methods, and tools described in *Risk Management Revisited*.   Of course I recommend reading all of *Risk Management Revisited* as a prerequisite to *Survival Games*, but for those who haven't read *RMR* or would just like a quick refresher, here it goes.

The MFRA begins with a comprehensive search for hazards that could potentially produce mega fatality events.   This task was organized around the master logic diagram (MLD) shown below (slightly modified from the *RMR* version). From this search, 22 initiating events were selected for quantification.

Exhibit 1-1 MFRA Master Logic Diagram

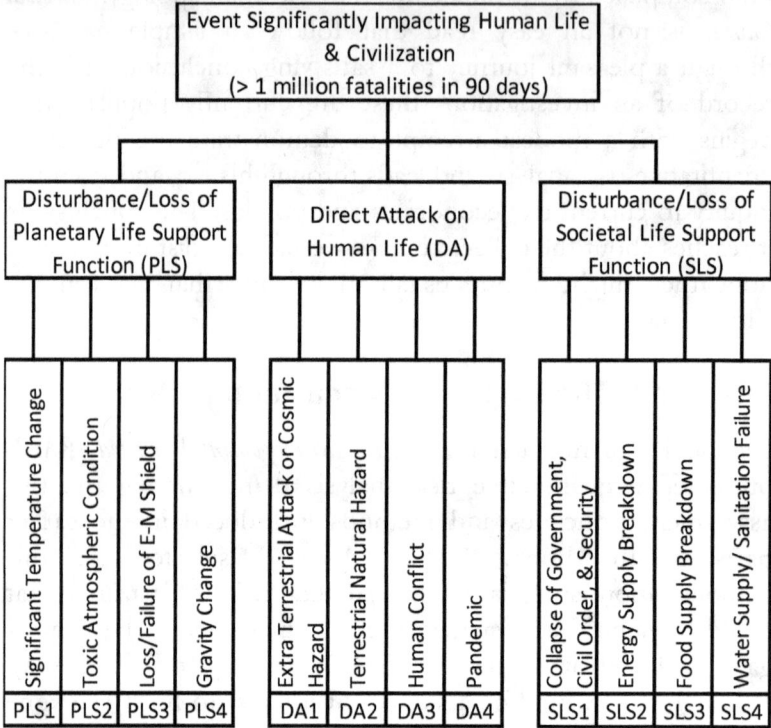

The quantitative Mega Fatality Risk Assessment (MFRA) was constructed using an event tree model consisting of 22 event trees, 33 event tree top events, and 31 end states. A total of 67 scenarios were quantified, including uncertainty, using *Excel/Crystal Ball* Monte Carlo simulation software. The overall architecture of the MFRA model is depicted in the following exhibit.

Exhibit 1-2 MFRA Model Architecture

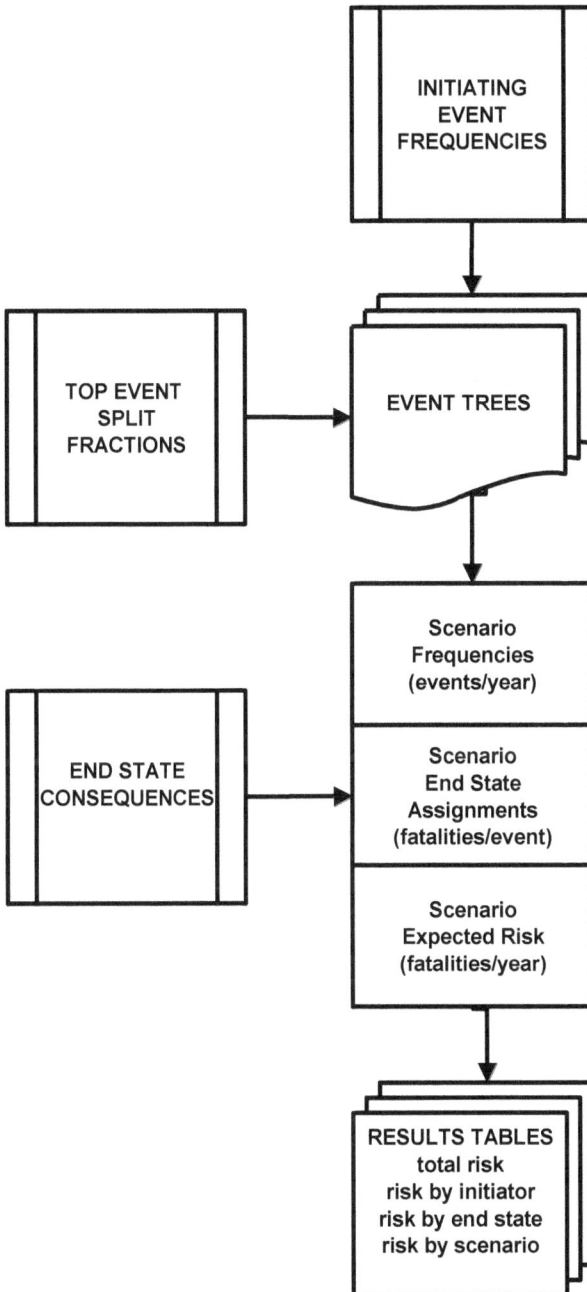

The bottom line result of MFRA is an estimate of the total prompt fatalities that would result from the examined sources of mega fatality risk. This result was, of course, in the form of a probability distribution which is shown below.

Exhibit 1-3 Expected Fatalities per Year

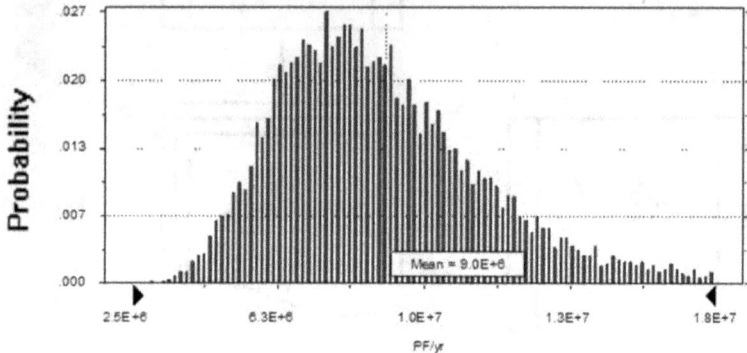

The mean value of this distribution is about 9.0 million expected fatalities per year. For a population of 7.2 billion people, this level of fatalities represents an individual risk of about 0.00125 per person per year or about 14% of the average individual fatality risk from all causes that we have actually experienced in recent times.

The following exhibit breaks down the contributors to mega fatality risk by event type.

Exhibit 1-4 MFRA Results Breakdown by Initiator

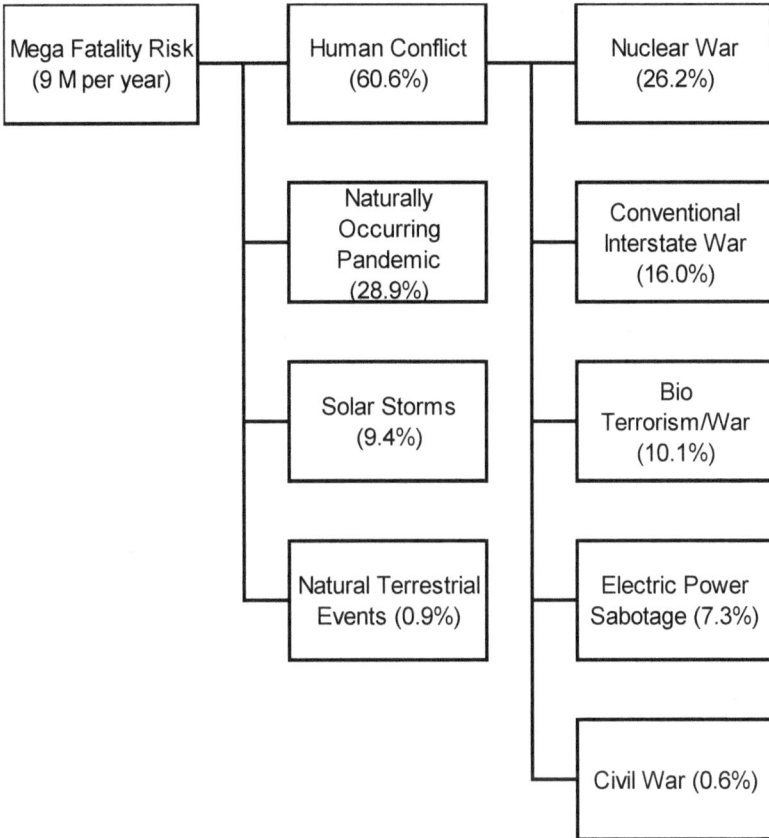

Mega Fatality Risk (9 M per year)	Human Conflict (60.6%)	Nuclear War (26.2%)
	Naturally Occurring Pandemic (28.9%)	Conventional Interstate War (16.0%)
	Solar Storms (9.4%)	Bio Terrorism/War (10.1%)
	Natural Terrestrial Events (0.9%)	Electric Power Sabotage (7.3%)
		Civil War (0.6%)

Risk Management Revisited provides a much more comprehensive presentation and discussion of these results than I have summarized here and I urge you to look back and review *RMR* again if you have lingering questions about how it was performed or how your favorite existential risk topic was treated.

Beyond Risk Management Revisited

I paused after completing *RMR* to consider what project to take on next. Even before I retired from full time work, many colleagues asked me to write a definitive guide for project risk management. I pounded for years on the brick wall of bad project management practices and this subject is something I may someday take on even though I am under no illusion as how difficult it would be to make a difference in a field with so many people firmly set in their ways. Several times in *RMR* I discussed project risk management issues, but *RMR* was first and foremost about documenting basic principles and methods. I did think about using a project management example in Part IV, but I thought this would have limited appeal compared with existential risk.

But, since existential risk is the subject I chose for the risk assessment example in *RMR*, I felt that I should first look there and think about what I really learned from that exercise and what more I might be able to add to our understanding of the potential apocalypse. First of all, I am still surprised that no one had actually assembled an integrated quantitative assessment of mega fatality risk before me. To be sure some parts of the overall existential risk picture had been assessed in great depth, but other areas not much at all. In my final comments in *RMR*, I note that I deliberately kept the MFRA simple, at least from the perspective of one accustomed to big quantitative risk models. But what does this mean and did I imply that more could be done? The short answer is yes! In building large complex risk assessments, it is common to approach the task in several phases of increasing scope and depth of analysis and to let preliminary results from one phase inform the specification of efforts that would provide the greatest risk management benefits in subsequent phases. This process is summarized graphically in the following generic scope – depth diagram.

Exhibit 1-5 Example Scope-Depth Chart

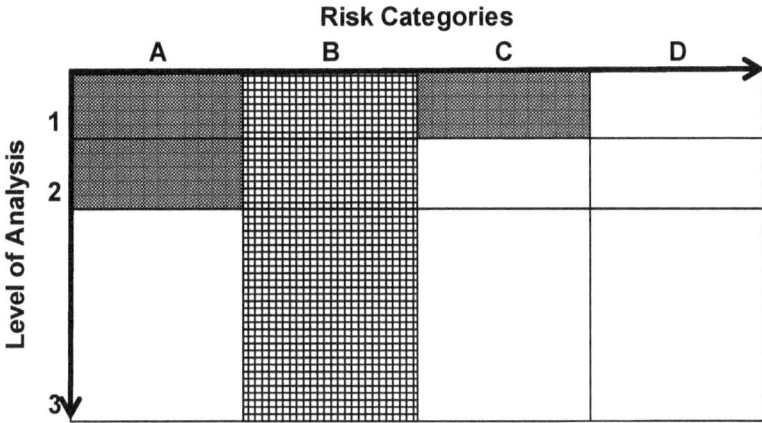

Level 1 - Qualitative analysis
Level 2 - Quantitative scoping analysis
Level 3 - Comprehensive quantitative analysis

What a chart like this tells us is how comprehensive the analysts believe their work is for each major category of risk included in the assessment. This particular example indicates that risk category A was assessed with a scoping level quantitative analysis. This means that informative quantitative results (level 2) were produced but the level of uncertainty remains higher than could be generated with a more robust level 3 analysis. If the results for this risk category are acceptable to those managing the risk, then time and effort have been saved in this risk category that can be applied to greater benefit in another area. The example further tells us that all possible effort was expended to examine risk category B. Some event related to this risk category may have been the reason the analysis was undertaken in the first place. The chart also tells us that risk category C only received a qualitative review and that risk category D was not included in this phase of work.

So, you may ask, what would the scope-depth chart look like for the MFRA? This is the subject of the next exhibit.

Exhibit 1-6 MFRA Scope-Depth Chart

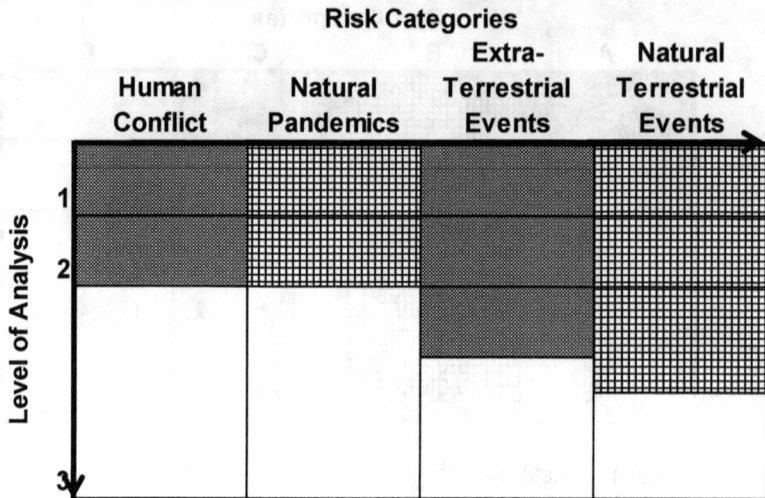

Level 1 - Qualitative analysis
Level 2 - Quantitative scoping analysis
Level 3 - Comprehensive quantitative analysis

Again, the aim of the MFRA was to demonstrate basic quantitative risk analysis concepts and methods. To do this, a level 2 scoping analysis across all important risk categories was my objective. However, my research for the MFRA yielded some very comprehensive work already done by others that I could readily utilize to produce better than level 2 analyses in the areas of extraterrestrial risk and especially for natural terrestrial hazards like earthquakes and volcanoes. For the biggest contributors to total risk, however, I had to produce the original work you see in *RMR*. This then begs the question of how the risk predicted by the MFRA might change and how the level of uncertainty in the risks might change if more robust analyses were performed.

This is a fair question and the results from exhibit 1-4 provide a guide for risk categories where additional effort should be invested if more robust results are desired. So what could be done to turn up the microscope and get more comprehensive results?

First, let's recognize that there are two fundamental approaches that can be used to estimate the occurrence of future events. The first is the statistical or actuarial approach where relevant historical data is examined and an assessment is made of the confidence with which future events can be predicted by extrapolating past experience into the future. The second approach requires the analyst to understand the physics of how an event of interest occurs and then to use this knowledge to mathematically model the relevant processes that produce the event under study. If known, physics models can produce much more reliable predictions of future performance than statistical analyses. Of course, this choice of approaches is not black and white. Even if the physics of a problem is well known, good data for the input conditions to the physics model are still essential to obtaining good predictions of future performance. And, this physics input data is often very valuable for risk management because it can indicate developing conditions before they result in a catastrophic event. For example, with an understanding of the physics of volcanism, stress in and around a volcano can be measured to produce much better predictions of future eruptions than would be possible with only statistical extrapolation.

For the events listed in exhibit 1-4, solar storm was the only event that had any real physics behind the estimates of frequency and consequences. The expected frequencies of terrorism, pandemics, and human conflict in the MFRA were all based on extrapolations of historical data into the future. The MFRA end states for conditional fatalities were defined using a parametric approach that combined estimates of the affected population and an estimate of the conditional lethality for the affected population. Each event tree scenario was then assigned to a representative end state.

However, I was more comfortable with the use of this approach for pandemics than human conflict. The future risk from pandemics is being driven by a race between increasing population, population density, and ever more rapid means of travel that are increasing global risk and advancing medical science and health provider capabilities which are decreasing pandemic risk. These two forces now battle to a near draw and this condition may continue indefinitely. Thus, extrapolating from recent history for pandemic frequency and consequences will probably yield reasonable results.

Human conflict and terrorism are another story, however. In *RMR*, I did some basic data research to estimate the frequency of conflicts occurring and then projected that any conventional conflict had some small chance of escalating into a nuclear conflict. Also, *RMR* estimated the consequences of all events, including conflicts, with the same parametric approach. No physics based end states were developed.

As I will discuss in the chapters that follow, further research on human conflict quickly led me to conclude that additional work might produce different results and, more importantly, much better insights into what the drivers of human conflict risk in the 21st century are and how they could be avoided or at least better limited.

As a result, the focus of *Survival Games* can be defined by the following risk assessment scope-depth chart.

Exhibit 1-7 Focus Area for Survival Games

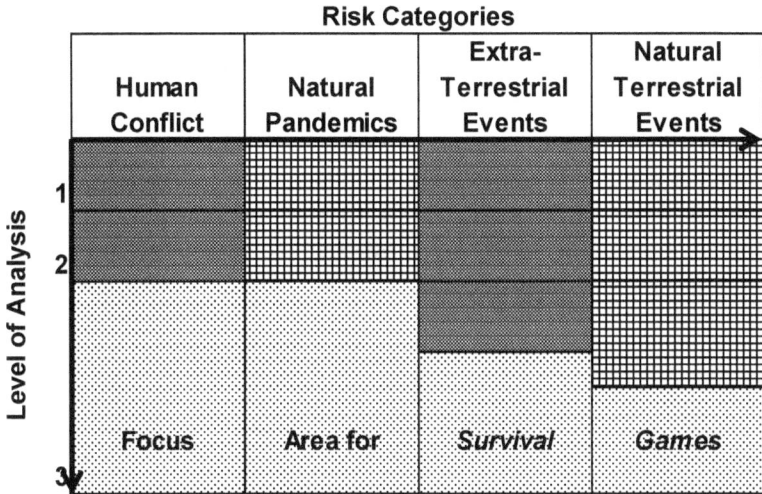

Risk Categories

	Human Conflict	Natural Pandemics	Extra-Terrestrial Events	Natural Terrestrial Events

Level of Analysis

Focus   Area for   Survival   Games

Level 1 - Qualitative analysis
Level 2 - Quantitative scoping analysis
Level 3 - Comprehensive quantitative analysis

But beyond diving deeper into the quantitative analysis of mega fatality risk, I felt that I might also be able to better explain the context in which an individual person or a leader responsible for more than just his or her own personal safety should judge the importance of these risk results.

In the end, these considerations led me structure *Survival Games* around the following three questions.

1. If I turned up the microscope on the important existential risk contributors found in the MFRA, will I discover any new and important findings that would change the first phase results and/or conclusions?

2. Do mega fatality events represent a risk that ordinary people should pay any attention to?

3. Is there anything an ordinary person can do to reduce their exposure to mega fatality risk?

The research I have done to answer the first question comprises Parts II, III, and IV of this book and is followed by a presentation of the updated MFRA results in Part V. Questions 2 and 3 are answered in Part VI. Data from all earlier work is used in Chapter 20 to provide a format for answering question 3 that can be used by each reader to customize their own specific risk management actions.

Enjoy the journey!

Part II - The History of Warfare

Chapter 2 - The Long War

War in the MFRA

So let's begin by taking a closer look at how war was modeled in the MFRA. In *RMR*, I structured the MFRA so that I could distinguish "normal" warfare from war initiated by terrorism or economic collapse. This was because I thought that nations were collectively less well prepared to address terrorist acts or a global economic crash as a source of potential conflict than they were the old fashioned territorial and other types of disputes that have caused past wars. In other words, terrorism might be more likely to cause future wars than the past initiators. But when building the event trees to incorporate this idea into the MFRA, I came to the conclusion that both the old and the new sources of conflict could end up at the same place. To handle this and still be able to distinguish between the various possible initiators, I elected to define general categories of warfare as end states and then built event trees that would allow different scenarios with different initiators to take separate paths to these common warfare end states. The architecture for this approach is illustrated in the following exhibit.

Exhibit 2-1 MFRA Architecture for War Modeling

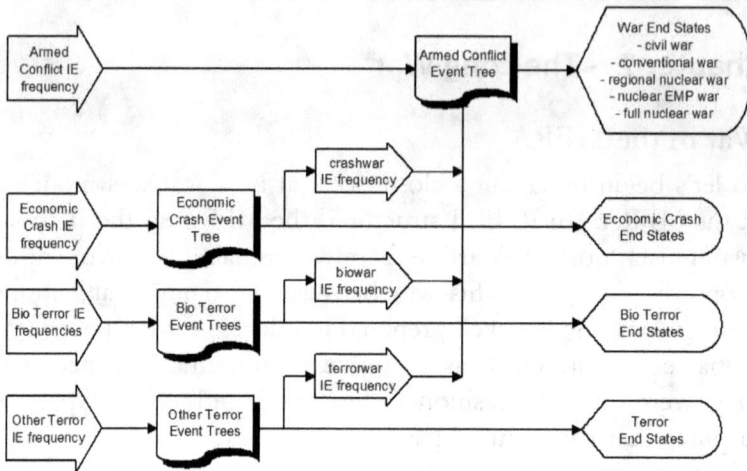

As you can see, the initiating event (IE) from which all war end states came was called "armed conflict" and all scenarios whether they began as "normal" wars or terrorist events or an economic crash were routed through this event tree where the severity of the conflict was assessed.

The initiating event frequency for armed conflict or "armcon" was developed from data for all wars that occurred between World War II and the terrorist attack on 9/11/2001. I felt this period would provide the most representative data for future conflicts not caused by terrorism. The probability distribution for this value turned out to have a mean value of 3.03 events per year.

The armed conflict event tree then sorted out this initiating event frequency into the nine "wardeaths" end states. The mean value of the prompt fatalities expected from these end states ranged from 20,000 for wardeaths1 to 1.4 billion for wardeaths9. Averaged over all end states, the mean expected prompt fatalities for all war scenarios was about 1.2 million per war.

So now let's take a deeper dive into the available data on the frequency and consequences of war and see if we can sharpen the results produced by the MFRA

Data on Warfare

Let's start by expanding our examination of historical data on warfare from the shorter modern era used for the MFRA to look at the full scope of available data. To do this I searched for more comprehensive data sources and found some really interesting work that has been done by others. But in tracing back the references in this work, the following databases cataloging data on both the duration and fatalities of wars were especially useful:

- The Conflict Catalog 18 vars, compiled by Peter Brecke for The Peace Science Society (International) and administered by the Department of Political Science at the Pennsylvania State University.
- The Armed Conflict Dataset, compiled by Lacina, Bethany & Nils Petter Gleditsch for the Peace Research Institute Oslo (PRIO) at Uppsala University.
- Wars and Casualties of the 20th and 21st Centuries by Piero Scaruffi

Both these databases provide a comprehensive list of conflicts that have occurred since the end of World War II. But the Brecke data also includes data on the duration and causalities for wars dating back to AD 1400! This is an incredible piece of work and one that, no doubt, will never be complete. The following data presented here is derived from these sources, unless otherwise noted. As a word of caution, I must note that this data is imperfect; differences such as the definitions of what conflicts should be counted make any analysis difficult. For this work, I used only events where data on both occurrence and fatalities was presented.

The Frequency of Conflict

Although the Conflict Catalog provides a good list of wars dating back to AD 1400, there was a notable sparsity of fatalities data for conflicts prior to about AD 1800. As a result, I used the period from 1800 to the present for this analysis. The following exhibit shows the number of conflicts that started in each decade between 1800 and 2010.

Exhibit 2-2 Conflicts per Decade

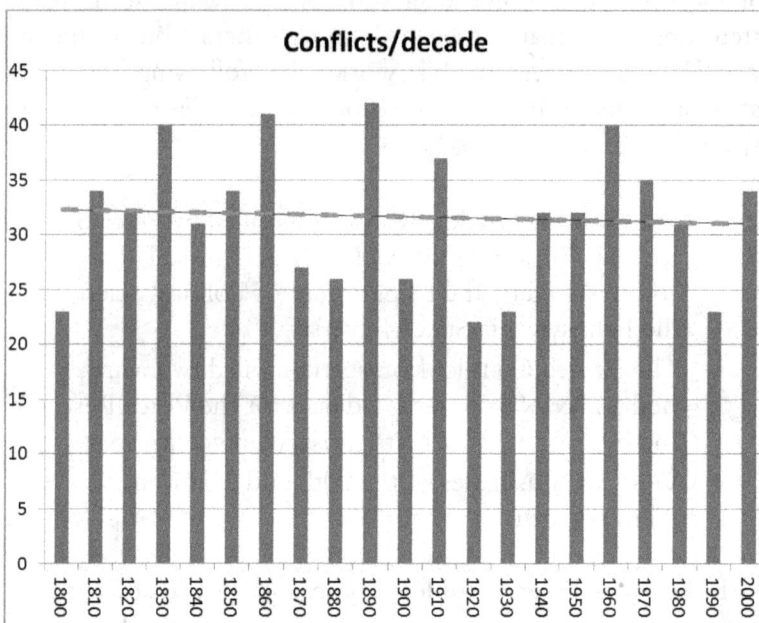

Observe that there is certainly variability in this data but the long term dashed trend line is nearly flat over 210 years, indicating that the frequency of conflicts is not changing significantly with time. The average over this 210 year period is 31.67 conflicts per decade compared with the mean of 30.3 used in the MFRA. Thus, the broader data search seems to confirm that the MFRA initiating event frequency for armed conflict was pretty good.

But let's dig even a little deeper for possible insight from the data. As we will discuss later, many political scientists argue that, at least since WWII, war is becoming obsolete and that humans are maturing into more peaceful, enlightened creatures. But does the above data support this claim? I said that the trend line above looks flat, but if we calculate the average conflict rates before and after WWII, we see that the conflict rate is actually showing a slight increase!

1800 to 1950	31.33 conflicts/decade
1950 to 2010	32.5 conflicts/decade
MFRA	30.3 conflicts/decade

Thus, at least when it comes to starting conflicts, humans don't seem to maturing all that much. But to fully understand this picture, we also need to examine the consequences that result from conflict.

The Consequences of Conflict

As I mentioned before, a requirement that I had for database selection was that the data cover both the frequency and consequences of conflict. This is because both metrics will be needed later to attempt an update to our assessment of mega fatality risk. Thus, we can now examine the data sources cited previously for consequences as measured by military and civilian fatalities.

One issue I need to address up front is the use of absolute verses relative fatality measures. A quick look at the available information on war casualties reveals that many political scientists like to present fatalities data in terms of the fraction of the current population killed in conflicts. This is certainly a meaningful approach to use and, it has the advantage of presenting a dramatically improving (decreasing) rate for war deaths. But this result may be produced by the rapidly expanding population rather than by decreasing absolute numbers of war deaths. In either case, to make a quantitative assessment of risk, we need to estimate fatalities per conflict, which we will also do.

First, let's compile the data in terms of deaths per decade in order to provide a direct comparison with Exhibit 2-2.

Exhibit 2-3 Conflict Fatalities by Decade 1800-2010

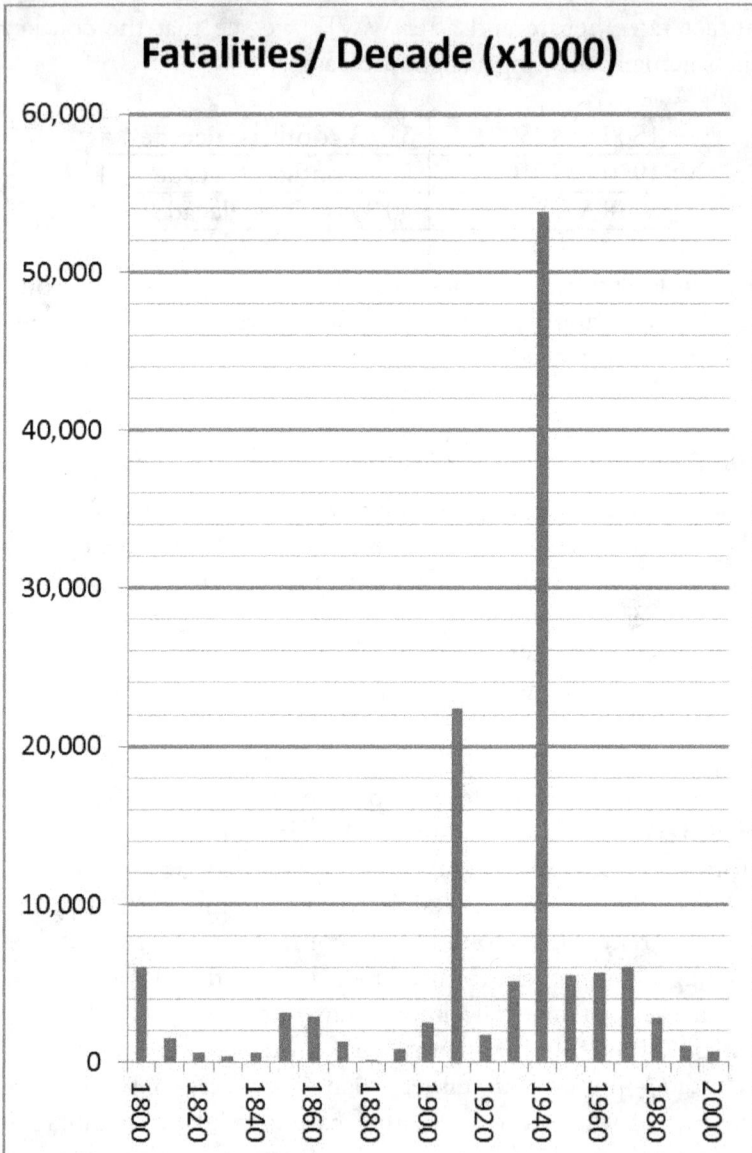

Fatalities/ Decade (x1000)

The next exhibit shows the same data in terms of the percentage death rate for the available population.

Exhibit 2-4 Conflict Death Rates 1800-2010

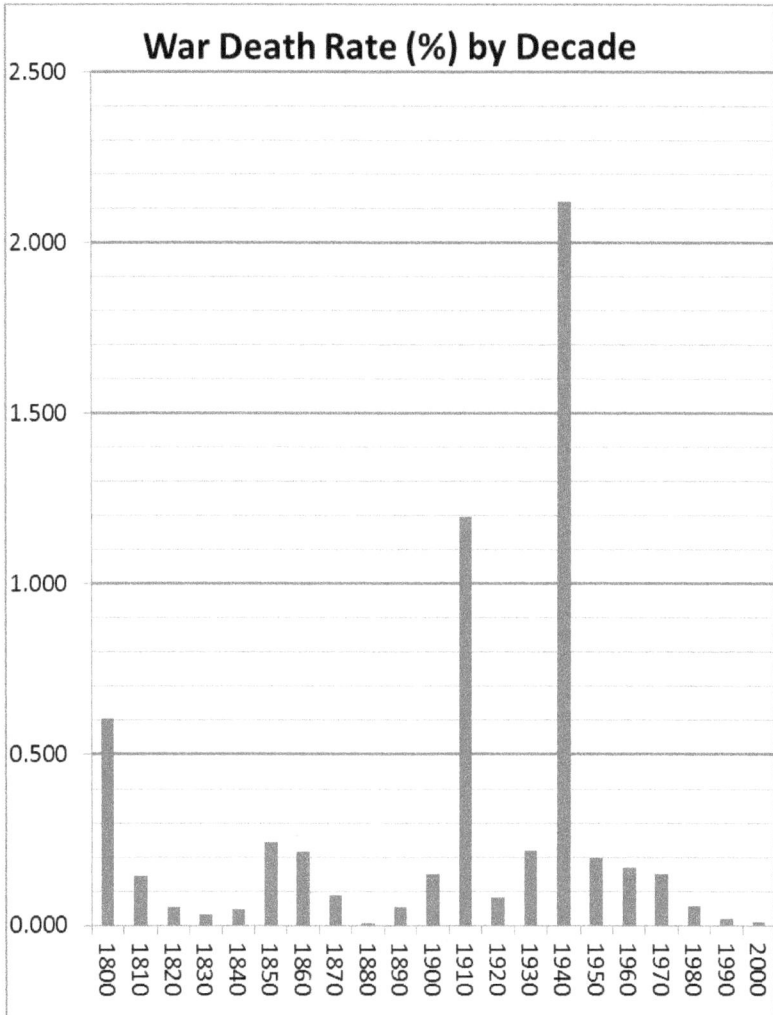

War Death Rate (%) by Decade

This perspective tends to make conflict deaths look more severe before WWII and less so in the years that follow.

In either case, it is obvious that the fatality data has much higher variability than the frequency data and is dominated by the conflagrations of the Napoleonic Wars, WWI, and WWII. There has been a marked decrease in conflict fatalities since

WWII, but two lengthy low fatality periods were also observed in the nineteenth century.

We are not yet ready to build end states to update our assessment of mega fatality risk, but if we took this data on historical war deaths and built a histogram of frequency and severity per conflict this would be the result.

Exhibit 2-5 Histogram of Fatalities per Conflict

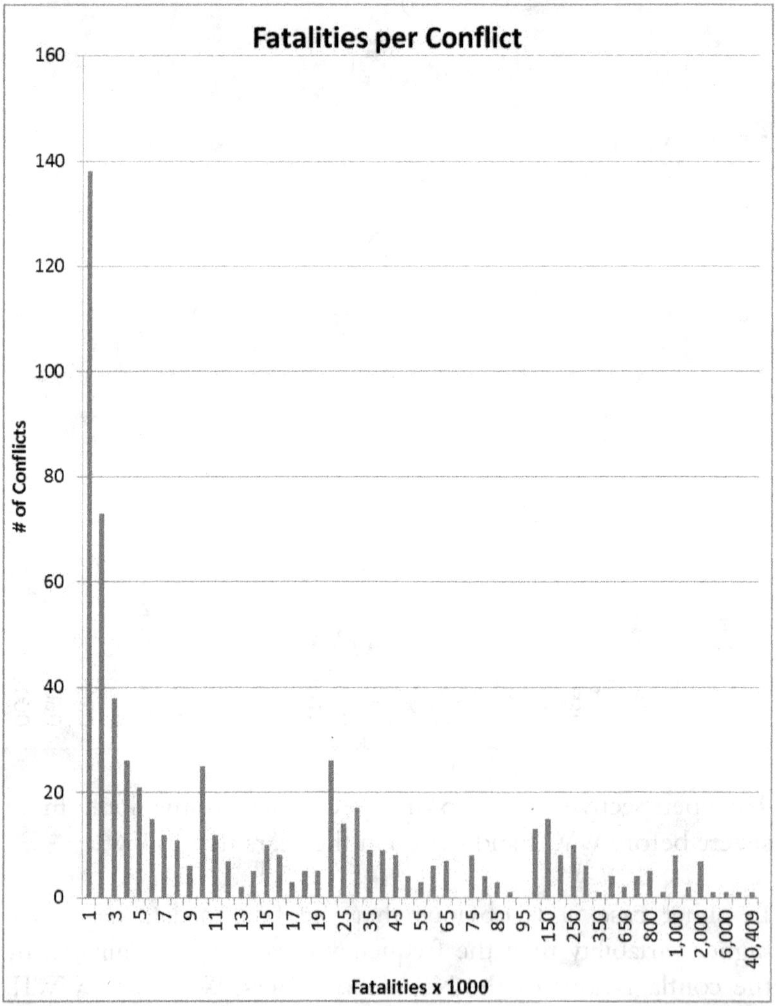

If we were to then develop a probability distribution that represents this data, it would be extremely right skewed with a mean value of about 194,000 fatalities per conflict but a median (50%tile) of only 7,000. If we then multiply this mean of 194,000 fatalities per conflict by the historical average of 3.167 conflicts per year from above, we get an annual risk of about 615,000 fatalities per year. From Exhibit 1-4 we can see that this is only about 40% of the risk predicted by the MFRA for conventional war (16% of 9 million = 1.44 million). Since the frequency of conflicts used in the MFRA was validated by the analysis above, this must mean that the consequences per conflict used in the MFRA are too high if historical experience is a good indicator of future performance.

But do you remember the large difference between the mean and median in the distribution for the historical data that I mentioned above? This represents a warning flag indicating that the historical data may only be good for predicting the future if the high fatality events we see at the right side of Exhibit 2-5 will recur to keep the strong skewness we observed in the data in place. If not, then the MFRA results may be over estimated by an even greater margin. So, let's take a closer look at these events.

Of the 630 conflicts listed on our database, nearly 60% resulted in less than 10,000 fatalities and only 20 are documented to be true mega fatality events with more than one million fatalities. These 20 mega conflicts are:

Exhibit 2-6 Mega Fatality Conflicts

Conflict	Description	Start	End	Total Fatalities
Afghan Civil War	Civil war with Russian intervention	1978	1999	1,000,000
Cambodian Communist Subjugation	Democide of opponents	1975	1979	1,900,000
China Taiping Rebellion	China	1850	1865	2,000,000
Chinese Civil War	Phase 1 civil war	1927	1936	1,250,000
Chinese Civil War	Phase 2 civil war + Japanese invasion	1937	1945	2,000,000
Chinese Civil War	Phase 3 civil war with U.S. intervention	1945	1949	1,000,000
Chinese Communist Subjugation	Democide of opponents	1950	1951	1,900,000
Genocide of Jews	German massacre of Jews	1941	1945	6,000,000
German Expulsion from Poland	Democide of Germans in Poland	1945	1948	1,585,000
Indochina War	Vietnam-France regional war	1946	1954	1,200,000
Korean War	N Korea (& China)- S Korea (& UN forces)	1950	1953	1,500,000
Lopez War	Paraguay-Brazil, Uruguay, & Argentina regional war	1864	1870	1,100,000
Napoleonic Wars	Napoleonic Wars	1803	1815	4,425,000
Nigerian Civil War	Biafra separation	1967	1970	1,100,000
Ottoman Rebellions	Genocide of Armenians	1915	1923	1,883,000
Spanish Revolution	Civil war with intervention by Germany & Italy	1936	1939	2,000,000
Sudanese Civil War	Democide of Southerners	1983	2005	1,000,000
Vietnamese War	Civil war with U.S. intervention	1964	1975	1,800,000
World War I	First World War	1914	1918	19,617,000
World War II	Second World War	1937	1945	40,409,000

Since these twenty events are very important to the overall fatality record, I performed a spot check to confirm the validity of this key data. For most of these events, the spot check confirmed the listed data. However, validation was not so easy for the six events that I classified as "democides". This refers to any event where a sovereign government deliberately murders its own citizens, usually using the condemnation of their race, religion, or political beliefs as justification. I found that in this class of events, only the Holocaust of the Jews by the Nazis to be well documented. For other such events I found that the fatality estimates varied significantly and that there were significant documented democide events not included in the conflict databases. By significant, I mean events with large enough numbers to more than double total fatality count. In *Death by Government*, R. J. Rummel documents the murder of 169 million people by their own governments in the twentieth century alone. Note that the uncertainty in democide fatalities is high with 169 million being Rummel's *mid-range estimate* that falls between the low of 76 million and the high of 359 million. The conflict database records only 14 million democide deaths among the twenty mega fatality events over a 210 year period. This is a big discrepancy.

Rummel also observed this discrepancy and in a complementary book, *Statistics of Democide*, he attempts to account for the differences between his work and the generally accepted data. His main hypotheses are:

- Many democide deaths are not recorded as war deaths because they did not result from military conflict. The victims were completely at the mercy of their authoritarian governments.
- Many democide deaths occurred by mass murder, but many more were caused by the deliberate application of starvation and disease.
- Significant numbers of the deaths attributed to war were actually civilians murdered by the deliberate acts listed above.

As a result, Rummel's accounting of conflict deaths during the twentieth century contrasts with the generally accepted data as follows.

Exhibit 2-7 Rummel vs Standard Fatalities data

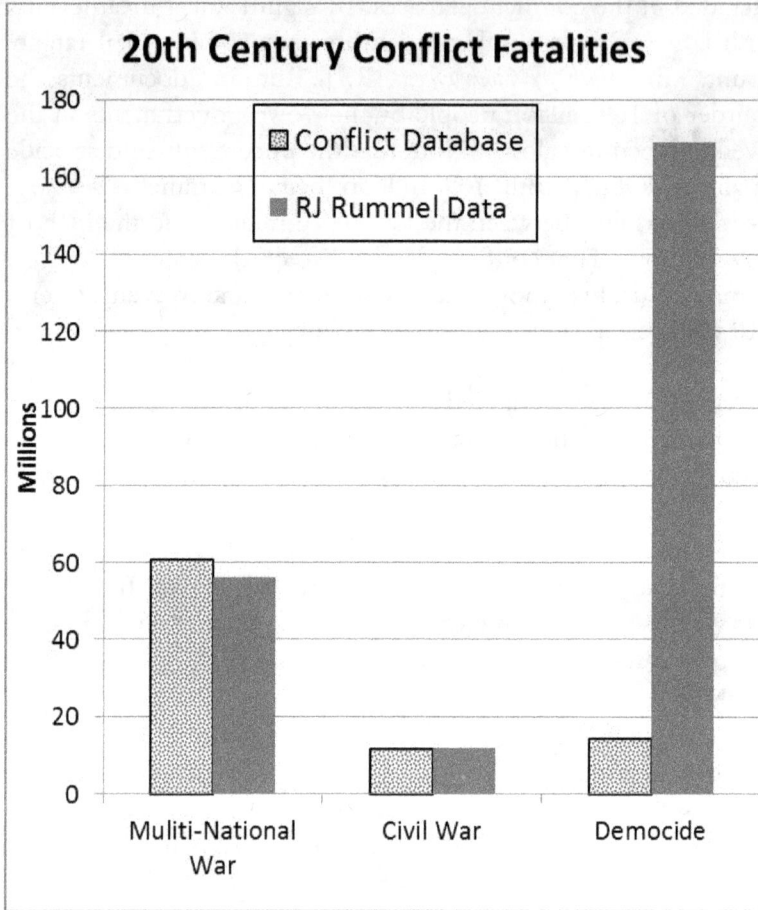

20th Century Conflict Fatalities

(chart legend: Conflict Database; RJ Rummel Data)

Y-axis: Millions (0 to 180)

X-axis categories: Muliti-National War; Civil War; Democide

Rummel's accounting includes 219 democide events over the period from 1900 to 1987 and produces 155 million more state sanctioned fatalities that the conflict data base. Most of the conflicts in Rummel's data are also included in the conflict data base. Thus, the frequency of conflict remains unchanged but the inclusion of democide deaths with war deaths greatly increases the mean fatalities per conflict from 194,000 to about 440,000 and raises the data derived war risk to about 1.4 million per year (3.167 x 440,000) or about 97% of the MFRA calculated risk for conventional war.

Like combat fatalities, the democide fatalities are dominated by several large events. More than 75% of all democide deaths were perpetrated by the totalitarian regimes of three countries: Nazi Germany, China, and the Soviet Union. It is also important to note that a significant number of the democide deaths occurred after WWII. This seems to contradict the generally accepted narrative that humanity is evolving away from violence. But since Rummel's data only extends through to 1987, we only have about four decades of comparative data to work with as shown below.

Exhibit 2-8 Democide & Combat Deaths Since WWII

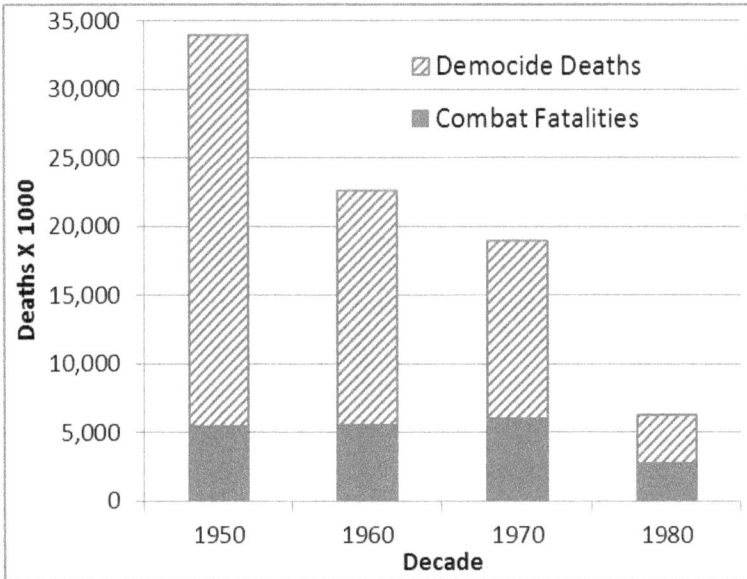

This chart shows the sharp drop in both combat and democide deaths after WWII, but the totals are dominated by democide.

The next exhibit shows the very latest data on conflict deaths since 2000. Here the 21st century seems to off to a very good start, but the accounting for democide in this data may not be complete and an uptick in the trend may be forming.

Exhibit 2-9 Combat Deaths Since 2000

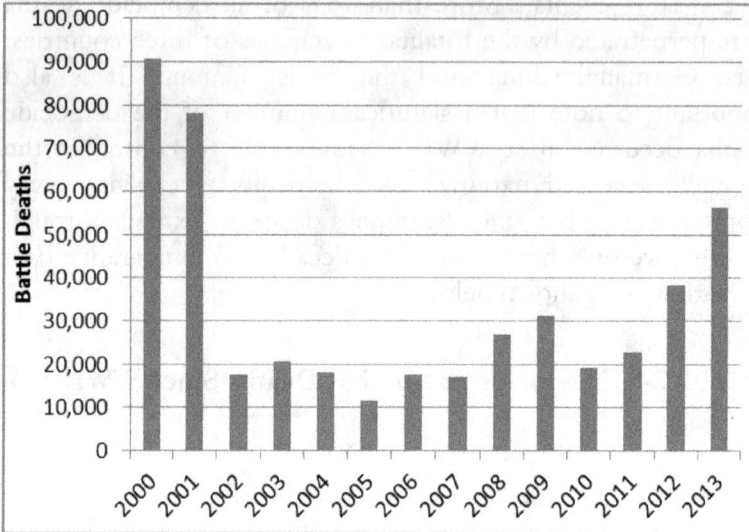

Conclusions

So far our examination of historical data has focused on the risk of conventional war and after many charts and tables my conclusion is that the risk calculated in the MFRA for conventional war is pretty well supported by a deeper evaluation of historical data. I'll say more about this in the next chapter but before we go on, let's remember that the MFRA also included an estimate of future risk from nuclear war.

Chapter 3 - The Long Peace

So what can we glean from all the data in Chapter 1 that can help to update our understanding of war risk? First let's list the findings that I think are important from the data analysis and then we'll take a closer look at what they tell us.

1. The frequency of conflicts that result in at least 1000 fatalities is remarkably consistent over a long period of time at about three per year and is not decreasing.

2. The median of the probability distribution for fatalities per conflict is also very consistent at somewhat less than 10,000 but the mean of this distribution is about than 50 times greater. This extreme difference between the mean and the median is characteristic of a strongly skewed probability distribution and is caused by a small number of mega fatality wars.

3. Since WWII, totalitarian regimes have dramatically reduced the scope and intensity of conflicts with other nation states, but have shown no hesitation to engage in mega fatality democides of their own people. Thus, since WWII, an individual's greatest risk of conflict death has come from their own government rather than interstate war.

4. The observed decline in annual battle deaths since WWII is the result of interstate conflicts ending without escalation to mega fatality outcomes (no WWIII). Future war risks will likely remain low if this trend continues. However, if a future conflict escalates to a nuclear conflict, the analysis in Part III indicates that the resulting fatalities could greatly exceed anything previously experienced and even threaten human extinction.

5. Thus, future war risk will be largely determined by the likelihood of nuclear war.

The data analysis convincingly shows that governments and other state like actors are not hesitating to initiate conflicts but have, so far, been able to prevent their escalation to nuclear conflict.

So what has caused this pattern of behavior? How does it operate to limit the scope of conflicts? What could happen to disturb this behavior and produce a nuclear conflict? These are the questions we need to answer before proceeding to assess risk.

You may be thinking that I did a lot of work to just arrive at the obvious. But remember from Risk Management Revisited that it is important to comprehensively document our state of knowledge before performing a risk assessment. But in addition, these findings may not be all that obvious to everyone. Many renowned academics, theologians, and others have tried to document and explain the same phenomena our data analysis has found. Let's take a brief look at what they say and compare their assessments with the data.

First a brief history of nuclear weapons proliferation. Following WWII the three signees of the original Quebec Agreement each had access to the nuclear technology developed by the Manhattan Project. The U.S. and Great Britain continued with the development of nuclear weapons but Canada refrained. With the detonation of their first test weapon in August 1949, the Soviet Union joined the nuclear weapons club and began the Cold War era which lasted until the collapse of the Soviet Union in 1991. The time since is referred to as the Post-Cold War era, but I think this label should only extend through to the Russian invasion of Ukraine in 2014. We are now in an era where the belligerence and nuclear threat of the Soviet Union has been effectively replaced by that of the Russian Federation. Although the U.S. and Russia are once again adversaries, their nuclear arsenals have been greatly reduced and are not on as high an alert status. But this improved condition is countered by the secondary or derivative nuclear weapons proliferations in India, Pakistan, North Korea, and Iran and the pall of Islamic Terrorism.

So what do the great thinkers of our time say about the prospects for war and peace in the nuclear era and how might we use their wisdom to advance our quantitative assessment of risk?

The Cold War Era

John Lewis Gaddis is generally recognized as the preeminent historian of the Cold War era. The title of this chapter "The Long Peace" is a phrase coined by Gaddis and used in his books including the definitive *The Cold War, A New History*. This phrase is used to emphasize the definitive change in behavior that has occurred since 1945. Europe has now been without war for 71 years, an era of peace not observed since at least the time of the Romans. Before 1945, war was so common it was considered inevitable. Gaddis' description of how this change happened is compelling and you should read it for yourself. The main conclusions, from his own words are:

"The leaders of these countries were probably no less belligerent than those who had resorted to war in the past, but their bellicosity lacked optimism: for the first time in history *no one* could be sure of winning, or even surviving, a great war. Like the barbed wire along the Hungarian border, *war itself -at least major wars fought between major states - had become a health hazard, and therefore an anachronism.*"

This new realization that war was no longer rational was implemented by a new code of conduct or rules of engagement that included; "avoiding direct military clashes, respecting existing spheres of influence, tolerating physical anomalies like the Berlin Wall and mental anomalies like the doctrine of Mutual Assured Destruction, refraining from efforts to discredit or undermine leaders on each side, and even a mutual willingness, through the new technology of reconnaissance satellites, to allow spying as long as it took place hundreds of miles above the earth."

In other words, through all of human history the making of war was, for leaders, a rational choice until suddenly, it was not. In Gaddis work, I sense no doubt about the role he believes nuclear weapons played, that's why he calls it *nuclear deterrence*.

The Post-Cold war Era

With the fall of the Soviet Union, the reunification of Germany, and the emergence of many new democratic governments many hoped that a new golden era of peace and prosperity was at hand. And, indeed, the evidence from the 1990's and early twenty first century seemed to confirm this belief. No one put this hope for a new era into better perspective than Steven Pinker, a Harvard psychologist who in 2011 published *The Better Angels of Our Nature – Why Violence has Declined*. In this best-selling book Pinker provides copious data (good work grad students!) selected to demonstrate that all forms of human violence are in decline.

Pinker's view of the role nuclear weapons have played in deterring war is clear. He states:

"If the Long Peace were a nuclear peace, it would be a fool's paradise, because an accident, a miscommunication, or an air force general obsessed with precious bodily fluids could set off an apocalypse. Thankfully, a closer look suggests that the threat of nuclear annihilation deserves little credit for the Long Peace."

Pinker then goes on at some length to claim that nuclear weapons cannot deter war because chemical weapons did not deter war. While his point that a nuclear weapon accident could occur is valid (see Chapters 8 & 9 of this book), his complete dismissal of nuclear deterrence is perhaps the most intellectually dishonest argument ever put to print. Nuclear weapons are vastly more destructive than chemical weapons (see my Chapter 5).

Pinker's general conclusions are, in my opinion, also undermined by selective cherry picking of the data and flawed reasoning. The decline in conflict deaths he weighs so heavily is, as the data shows, only the result of a reversion to the long term *median* of the distribution for fatalities per conflict (see Exhibits 2-3, 4 & 5). Although Pinker repeatedly states that a mega fatality conflict is still possible, he never acknowledges that the occurrence of just one such event would cause the data to revert to and perhaps extend beyond the long term *mean* for conflict deaths and this would totally destroy his overall hypothesis. I also question his reasoning because there is an obvious alternate hypothesis that could explain many of the data trends he documents. That hypothesis is that at every level of society - local, state, national, and international, there are more police on the job doing better police work that has ever been done before. So maybe human nature hasn't changed all that much.

Looking Forward

So what are we to expect from the future? The cold war between the U.S. and Russia has resumed to perhaps a chilly war but the landscape beyond these two nuclear powers is substantially different. There are no longer clear alliances delineating the spheres of influence for the two super powers. Old rules of behavior are not being observed with care. And, the U.S., Russia, and their closest allies are all the targets of Islamic terrorism. Will cold war style nuclear deterrence work to sustain peace going forward?

Let's begin the search for a comprehensive and objective answer to this question.

Chapter 3 References:

3-1. *The Cold War, A New History*, John Lewis Gaddis, The Penguin Press, 2005, ISBN 1-59420-062-9.

3-2. *The Better Angels of Our Nature – Why Violence has Declined*, Steven Pinker, Viking Penguin, 2011, ISBN 978-0-670-02295-3.

Part III – Consequences of Nuclear War

Use of the two atomic weapons that ended WWII clearly signaled the start of the nuclear era, but that experience presents only a glimpse of what the consequences of a full scale nuclear conflict would be. The MFRA used a simple parametric approach to estimate the scope of fatalities that could result from a nuclear conflict. To begin a more comprehensive evaluation of nuclear war risk, I believe that a more comprehensive look at the conditional consequences that would result if a nuclear conflict did occur is warranted. The question of frequency will be addressed later. Because the potential consequences of nuclear war are critical inputs at several points in this book, the results of this analysis may be referenced multiple times as we proceed.

The likelihood of nuclear war in the MFRA was calculated by allowing some chance that conventional conflicts escalate out of control and become nuclear conflicts. The MFRA scenarios leading to nuclear war were grouped into three possible end states representing a regional nuclear conflict (wardeaths5) a limited global conflict (wardeaths7) and an unlimited global war (wardeaths9). To provide a starting benchmark for our review of nuclear war risk, I have displayed the mean conditional consequences for these end states in the following table.

MFRA Nuclear War End States

MFRA End State	MFRA Mean Fatalities (millions)
wardeaths5	60
wardeaths7	420
wardeaths9	1400

But can we find a way to better estimate the deaths that would result from a nuclear conflict that has never happened? Let's try.

To make a more comprehensive assessment of consequences resulting from the use of nuclear weapons we will first summarize the types and numbers of weapons available. Then we will examine the effects that would result from the individual use of these weapons. This in turn begs the more difficult and more uncertain question of what the aggregate effects would be from the use of multiple weapons. With the answers to these questions in hand, we can then reexamine the appropriateness of the MFRA end states.

Chapter 4 - A Primer on Nuclear Weapons

The age of atomic or nuclear warfare began on July 16, 1945 with the detonation of the Trinity test device at Alamogordo, New Mexico. It was soon followed by the dropping of the Little Boy device over Hiroshima and the Fat Man device over Nagasaki that ended World War II. These first generation nuclear weapons derived their energy from the fission of special nuclear materials, Uranium 235 for Little Boy and Plutonium 239 for Fat Man. The explosive yields of these first weapons were about 15 kt and 20 kt respectively where kt stands for kilotons of TNT equivalent.

In the Cold War years that followed, scientists learned how to build more efficient and powerful devices that combined the fission process with the even more powerful fusion process to allow weapons to be built that produced yields in the multiple megaton range. The following exhibits attempts to illustrate the difference in power between conventional and nuclear explosives. In the first exhibit, I calibrated the vertical axis on a logarithmic scale allowing some of the lower yield devices to register. But on the second exhibit, I used a linear scale to more dramatically show the differences. If this still doesn't impress you, let me paint the following verbal image. If using the linear graph, I drew the bar representing the 2,000 pound conventional bomb to be one inch high, then the bar for the thermonuclear warhead would have to be over 41,000 feet high! It is understandable that the human mind has a difficult time comprehending the power of nuclear weapons.

Exhibit 4-1 Logarithmic Yield Comparison

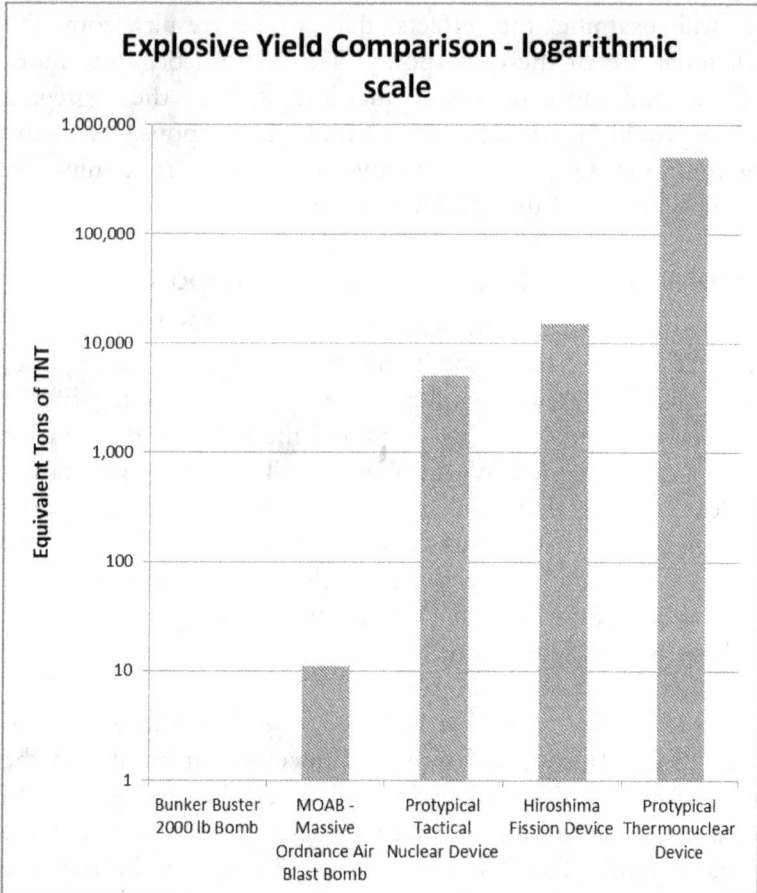

Explosive Yield Comparison - logarithmic scale

Exhibit 4-2 Linear Yield Comparison

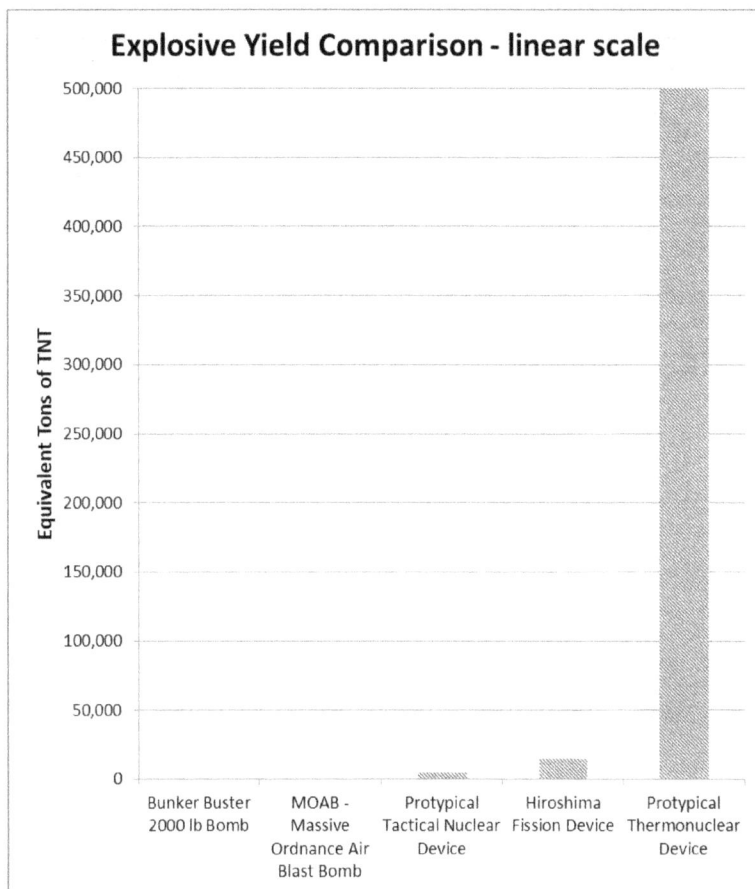

Explosive Yield Comparison - linear scale

[A bar chart titled "Explosive Yield Comparison - linear scale" with y-axis labeled "Equivalent Tons of TNT" ranging from 0 to 500,000 in increments of 50,000. The x-axis categories are: Bunker Buster 2000 lb Bomb; MOAB - Massive Ordnance Air Blast Bomb; Protypical Tactical Nuclear Device; Hiroshima Fission Device; Protypical Thermonuclear Device. Only the Hiroshima Fission Device (~15,000) and Protypical Thermonuclear Device (~500,000) show visible bars.]

During the Cold War, the Soviet Union and the United States constructed vast arsenals of nuclear weapons that totaled to over 60,000 at their peak in the 1980's. The break-up of the Soviet Union helped create an environment where negotiations have been successful in significantly reducing the number of nuclear weapons but both Russia and the U.S. still have large arsenals along with other nations as detailed in the following exhibit

Exhibit 4-3 Nuclear Weapons Arsenals

Nuclear Weapons Arsenals

Country	Strategic Deployed	Strategic Reserved	Tactical	Total Inventory	Type
Russia	1,790	2,700	6,000	10,490	Thermonuclear
United States	1,750	2,740	760	5,250	Thermonuclear
France	280	10	unknown	290	Thermonuclear
China	0	260	unknown	260	Thermonuclear
United Kingdom	120	95	unknown	215	Thermonuclear
Israel	0	80	unknown	80	Thermonuclear
Pakistan	0	130	unknown	130	Fission
India	0	120	unknown	120	Fission
North Korea	unknown	unknown	unknown	unknown	unknown
Iran	unknown	unknown	unknown	unknown	unknown
Totals	**3,940**	**6,135**	**6,760**	**16,835**	

Data sources: *Status of World Nuclear Forces*, Federation of American Scientists, 3/1/2016

Nonstrategic Nuclear Weapons, Amy F. Woolf, Congressional Research Service, 2/23/2015

Chapter 5 - Weapon Effects

Effects from Use of a Single Weapon

The consequences that would result from the use of even one of these weapons would be devastating. But to make an objective assessment of risk, we have to examine this question and think about the unthinkable. We of course know the consequences that resulted from the two actual instances where nuclear weapons were used in war. But Little Boy and Fat Man were relatively small fission weapons. To establish a benchmark for the use of a large thermonuclear weapon however, we have to rely on technical projections. One such analysis has been publically released in a report prepared for the U.S. Congress by the Office of Technology Assessment in May 1979. *The Effects of Nuclear War* (Ref 5-1) describes the consequences of several hypothetical single weapon and multi-weapon exchanges between the U.S. and the Soviet Union. One of the cases examined is the air burst of a one megaton weapon over Detroit, Michigan. The following exhibit summarizes the consequences calculated for this case plus Hiroshima and Nagasaki data.

Exhibit 5-1 Nuclear Weapon Fatality Estimates

	Hiroshima	Nagasaki	Detroit (1)
Weapon Yield (kt)	15	20	1,000
Area Population (x1000)	255-400	195-250	4,500
Total Fatalities (x1000)	66-150	39-80	220-2,500
Lethality	26-37%	20-32%	5-55%
Diameter of 50% lethality boundary (miles)	2	2	10

(1) *The Effects of Nuclear War*, U.S. Office of Technology Assessment, May 1979

The uncertainty in the Hiroshima and Nagasaki data comes from the fact that the bombings were real war time events and not controlled experiments. Key information such as the initial populations within the blast areas cannot be known with any great precision. The wide range of outcomes for the OTA analysis comes from acknowledgement that adverse weather and burst height variations can dramatically influence casualties. With use as intended, however, consequences can be expected to be at the high end of the stated ranges.

Aggregate Effects of Multiple Weapons Use

If the casualties caused by multiple nuclear weapons simply scaled up linearly from those described above for a single weapon, then this question would be straightforward to answer. Unfortunately, the effects of multiple weapons use would be far greater than multiplicative. An unlimited exchange of thousands of nuclear weapons between the U.S. and Russia would devastate both nations. Estimates from *The Effects of Nuclear War* predict that as high as **88% of the U.S. population would die** in such an exchange from direct weapons effects, without the consideration of ecological damage or long term health hazards. So, from a risk assessment perspective, this begs the question of what would be the short term and long term regional and global impacts of such a war and could widespread impacts be triggered by the use of smaller numbers of nuclear weapons? To answer these questions, I will discuss several relevant phenomena individually and then try to assemble a more complete picture of the integrated consequences.

Damage efficiency enhancement

Damage analyses like those presented in *The Effects of Nuclear War* demonstrated to war planners that a spread pattern of lower yield nuclear weapons much more effectively destroyed a target area than a single high yield weapon. This also allowed for a more efficient use of special nuclear materials and a more diverse array of delivery vehicles. In projecting fatalities, this meant that the percent lethality for a given target area could be significantly increased from the data presented in Exhibit 5-1.

Survival Games

Short term societal life support (SLS) system disruptions
The single weapon detonations produced large numbers of people that were injured in addition to those killed. Because of the limited size of the attack area, the still mobile injured were able to escape the damage zone and aid was able to move in from all directions to meet them. A broader scale attack will in itself make any early response more difficult but it will also disrupt the technological systems that modern society relies on to provide for the daily need of billions of people. Chief among these societal life support systems is electric power. Those critical facilities that have not been destroyed may have emergency power supplies that can operate for a few hours or days, but when their fuel supplies run out, resupply will not be possible and a new level of chaos will be experienced. This chaos will challenge the survival of even those outside the target area that are affected by SLS failure.

Long term societal life support system disruptions
Effects that begin to appear immediately after an attack but that may persist for months or years include the continued disruption of societal life support systems described above. Two additional phenomena that may cause regional and global consequences are radioactive contamination and climate change. The immediate target areas of the detonations will be severely contaminated but the level of devastation will generally mark the affected area to be avoided. Significant fallout that can be spread by the wind to contaminate areas outside the immediate target area is generally not produced by elevated air blast detonations. Also, actual experience with residual radiation exposure from Chernobyl and Fukushima has produced far fewer health effects that predicted by analyses. This is because the linear dose effects hypothesis used to make predictions of health effects for lower levels of radiation has been known for decades to be false. It continues to used, however, because there are powerful political groups with a vested interest in vastly overstating the projections of radiation hazards from nuclear power generation. Thus, residual radiation will be a serious hazard for survivors but only one of many that they will need to deal with.

Survival Games

The more serious long term phenomena potentially affecting wide areas is smoke induced climate change also referred to as a *nuclear winter*. There is no doubt that fine dust injected high into the atmosphere can cause significant cooling on a regional and global scale. This phenomenon, caused by an asteroid strike, is believed to have played a role in the extinction of the dinosaurs and was actually experienced on a smaller scale in 1816 following the eruption of Mount Tambora. Speculation about the ability of nuclear weapons to cause a global winter event first gained public attention when a group led by the late Carl Sagan published a paper on the subject in 1983. Some may have thought this risk was reduced or even eliminated by the SALT weapons reduction agreements, but recent analyses with better climate modeling tools indicates that significant global cooling could be initiated by the detonation of as few as 100 Hiroshima size (15kt) nuclear weapons (Ref 5-2 & 5-3). These analyses also show that the cooling experienced is dependent on the mass of dust generated, so the modest cooling (2.3^0F) caused by 100 weapons would not be the doomsday event (70^0F from 5000MT) predicted by Sagan, but it still could be a devastating event for billions of people if agricultural production is disrupted for even one year. The authors of this work obviously feel that any nuclear war is unacceptable, but for our assessment of risk, we need to make an assessment of the fatalities that would result from different levels of nuclear war that is as objective as possible. Since the affected population for a nuclear winter event is all humanity, a severe nuclear winter would be a complete or near complete extinction event. But even a nuclear winter of lesser severity could still kill billions. For defining end states to be used in updating MFRA results, we will assume the onset of nuclear winter consequences to begin with the use of 100 weapons and the possibility of human extinction to begin with the use of 3000 or more nuclear weapons. For conflicts that may fall in between these thresholds, an intermediate level of consequences will be used. This approach to end state definition is summarized in the following exhibit.

Exhibit 5-2 Gradations of Nuclear Winter

Gradations of Nuclear Winter			
Level	Weapons Used	Max Cooling (^{0}C)	Global Lethality (%)
Moderate	100-1000	1-4	10-50
Severe	1000-3000	4-8	50-90
Catastrophic	>3000	>8	99+

Based on the stockpile inventories reported earlier, a catastrophic nuclear winter would require the use of the American and/or Russian arsenals. Nuclear wars not involving Russia or America would still be capable of producing a moderate nuclear winter event.

EMP and Special Weapons

In addition to the phenomena already discussed, there are some special types of damage that can be created with nuclear weapons. Speculation about neutron weapons that could kill people with only minimal structural damage and cobalt bombs that would produce persistent lethal levels of radiation have made for some great science fiction but are not considered real threats. One special purpose weapon is of great concern however. The energy from a nuclear weapon detonated at a high altitude will react with the Earth's atmosphere and magnetic field to produce an electro-magnetic pulse (EMP) that will affect a target area on the surface hundreds of miles in diameter. All unshielded electrical and electronic equipment and devices within the target area will be shocked and potentially damaged beyond repair. The actual EMP phenomena and the reactions of electrical and electronic equipment to it is quite complex. Two reports (Ref 5-4 & 5-5) produced by a Presidential Commission created to examine this problem provide a comprehensive description of what could happen and some recommended risk reduction actions. The bottom line, however, is that an actual EMP attack against the USA would produce severe and long lasting damage to our society.

One of the most critical electrical components known to be vulnerable to EMP or other surge inducing stresses is high voltage power transformers. These large and normally very reliable devices (they have no moving parts) change alternating current voltages up and down in AC electric power systems. They are located in power plants and electric substations everywhere and their internal windings can be physically destroyed by EMP induced currents. One rumored classified analysis (Ref 5-6) is reported to show that the entire American electric power grid could be brought down with the simultaneous failure of as few as *nine* of these transformers in critical locations. Replacing any significant number of them would take months or years even with an all-out emergency effort. This is because they are normally very reliable and, as a result, few spares are kept on hand. Also, with the decline of U.S. manufacturing capability, very little domestic large transformer manufacturing capacity remains.

Although people are not directly harmed by an EMP event, the casualties that could result from a prolonged disruption of electric power systems, communication systems, and electronic controls of all sorts could be enormous. In the MFRA, I described such an event as a societal life support systems (SLS) failure and estimated the fatalities that could result by specifying probability distributions for the potential population at risk and a mortality rate for that population. Because the target area for an EMP attack could cover an entire continent, the mortality fraction does not have to be very high to produce a large number of fatalities. The estimates of fatalities in the MFRA are mine; I found no referenceable work by others upon which to base such numbers. The EMP Presidential Commission charged with evaluating this risk only makes the following comment on potential fatalities in its public report:

"It is possible for the functional outages to become mutually reinforcing until at some point the degradation of infrastructure could have irreversible effects on the country's ability to support its population."

Public comments made by several of those who served on the EMP Commission, however, reveal that there are in fact three classified report volumes and that they indicate that an EMP event could kill 60% to 90% of the U.S. population (Ref 5-7 & 5-8)! As a result, the end state distributions I will develop later in Chapter 15 will be based on these estimates.

Chapter 5 References:

5-1. *The Effects of Nuclear War*, U.S. Congress Office of Technology Assessment, May 1979.

5-2. Local Nuclear War - Global Suffering, Alan Robock and Owen Brian Toon, *Scientific American*, 2009

5-3. *Climatic Consequences and Agricultural Impact of Regional Nuclear Conflict*, Rutgers University presentation, Alan Robock, et al., 10/9/2012

5-4. Report of the Commission to Assess the Threat to the United States from Electromagnetic Pulse (EMP) Attack, Graham, et al, 2004

5-5. Report of the Commission to Assess the Threat to the United States from Electromagnetic Pulse (EMP) Attack, Graham, et al, 2008

5-6. U.S. Risks National Blackout From Small-Scale Attack, Rebecca Smith, *The Wall Street Journal*, 3/12/2014

5-7. "Electromagnetic Pulse: Threat to Critical Infrastructure", Dr. Peter Vincent Pry Testimony Before The Subcommittee on Cybersecurity, Infrastructure Protection and Security Technologies, House Committee on Homeland Security, 5/8/2014

5-8. Testimony of Dr. Michael J. Frankel to the House Homeland Security Committee Hearing Sub-Committee On Cyber Security, Infrastructure Protection, And Security Technologies, May 8, 2014

Chapter 6 - Defining End States for Nuclear War

So if we intend to update the MFRA results to reflect a better understanding of nuclear war consequences, what should we use for end state categories? With the information presented in this chapter, we can now use the type and number of nuclear weapons detonated to develop end state categories that match the characteristics of the scenarios produced from the likelihood analysis. The baseline data we will use to do this is summarized in the following exhibit.

Exhibit 6-1 Baseline Nuclear War Consequence Estimates

Nominal Baseline Data for Developing Nuclear War End States					
Effects	Damage Type	Weapons Used	Target population (x10E6)	Lethality	Fatalities (x10E6)
Direct Effects	EMP attack	1	100	5%	5
	Tactical attack on military	1	0.1	50%	0.05
	Strategic attack on populations	1	1	33%	0.33
Aggregate Effects	Enhanced SLS failure from multiple strategic weapons	n/a	1	20%	0.2
	Moderate Nuclear Winter	100-1000	7200	10%	720
	Severe Nuclear Winter	1000-3000	7200	50%	3600
	Catastrophic Nuclear Winter	>3000	7200	99.9%	7192.8

To provide a preliminary conclusion for this analysis, I will now compare the mean conditional consequences used for the three nuclear war end states defined in the MFRA with the fatality estimates developed above for moderate, severe, and catastrophic nuclear winter events. The results are shown in the following exhibit.

Exhibit 6-2 Preliminary Nuclear War Risk Update

MFRA End State	MFRA End State Fatalities (millions)	Updated Fatality Estimates (millions)	% of MFRA Risk
wardeaths5	60	720	1200%
wardeaths7	420	3600	857%
wardeaths9	1400	7200	514%

This exercise shows that the higher conditional fatality estimates presented in column 3 would increase the MFRA calculated risk for nuclear war by about an order of magnitude. This is an important preliminary finding, but be aware that it is based on MFRA war frequencies and a reexamination of that data will be our next area of inquiry.

Part IV - Nuclear War Likelihood

Chapter 7 - The Path to Nuclear War

So far, our main finding from the data and analyses in Chapters 2, 3, and Appendix A is that the overall war risk for the future will be largely determined by the risk of nuclear war, especially a nuclear war in which the number of weapons used is sufficient to initiate a nuclear winter. Nuclear weapons use sufficient to produce a nuclear winter would result from an exchange of weapons fired by two or more nuclear weapons states. It is inconceivable that any nuclear power would launch a large scale nuclear assault against a non-nuclear state.

But an exchange of nuclear weapons would have to begin with the detonation of the first weapon. So, let's break down this big question of how nuclear war could start into manageable size pieces and then examine each piece as best we can before reassembling the individual pieces into a whole. We showed how to do this in *Risk Management Revisited,* so we will resort to those tried and tested methods. Once again we will organize the risk assessment effort with the construction of a master logic diagram (MLD). Since by definition, a nuclear war requires the use of nuclear weapons, we will make nuclear weapon detonation our top event and chart the logical paths that could cause this to happen. The resulting MLD is shown in the next exhibit.

Exhibit 7-1 MLD for Nuclear Weapon Detonation

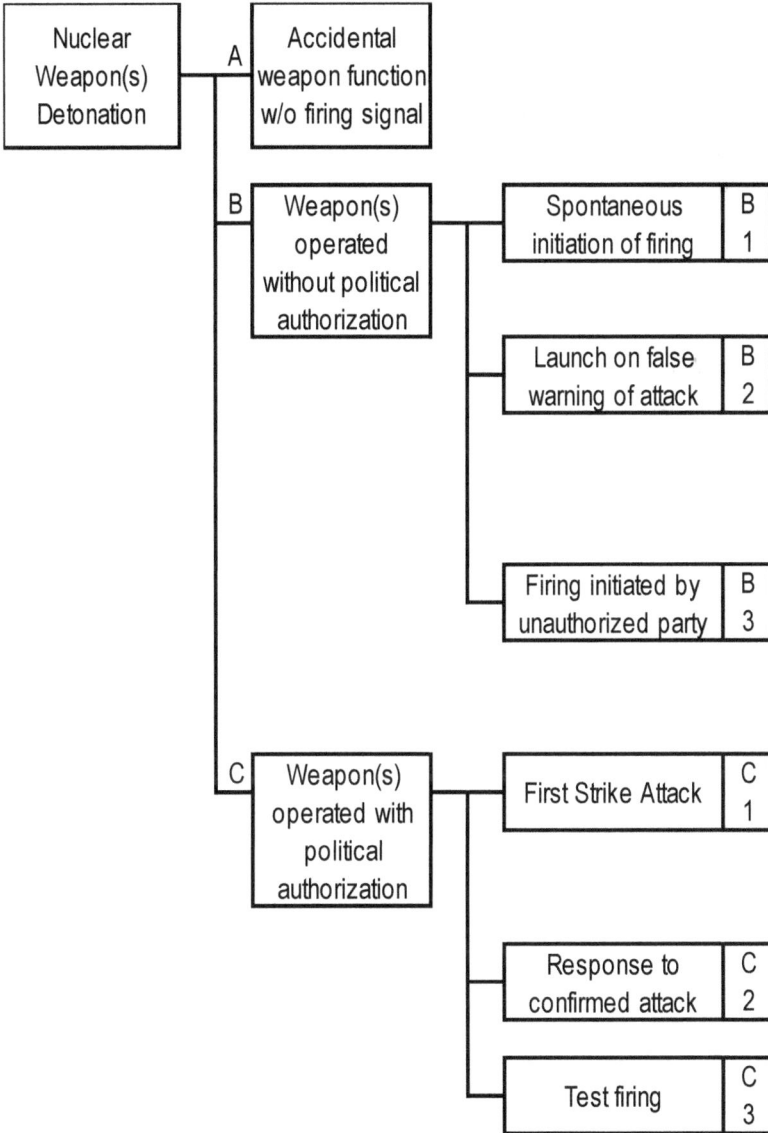

```
┌──────────────┐    ┌──────────────┐
│ Nuclear      │  A │ Accidental   │
│ Weapon(s)    │────│ weapon       │
│ Detonation   │    │ function     │
│              │    │ w/o firing   │
│              │    │ signal       │
└──────────────┘    └──────────────┘
```

B	Weapon(s) operated without political authorization	
		Spontaneous initiation of firing — B1
		Launch on false warning of attack — B2
		Firing initiated by unauthorized party — B3
C	Weapon(s) operated with political authorization	
		First Strike Attack — C1
		Response to confirmed attack — C2
		Test firing — C3

Note that the Detonation MLD does not say anything about the number of weapons detonated or the size or type of weapon. This information would come from an examination of the scenarios that feed into each MLD path. We will address that task later. But remember the purpose of a MLD is to chart all the logical paths that can produce the top event. This demonstrates the completeness of the assessment. Further evaluation can then focus on the frequency and consequence of each path, for which there may be significant uncertainty. From RMR, we also know how to use the language of probability to describe our state of knowledge about the uncertainty.

Let's go ahead.

In the next three chapters we will examine each of the three second level pathways identified in the Detonation MLD and discuss the important types of scenarios that would feed into each path.

Chapter 8 - Accidental Nuclear War

Before beginning an examination of the MLD paths, some further explanation of the top event is needed. For this exercise, nuclear weapon detonation is defined to be the functioning of a nuclear device that produces and explosive yield greater than that of the conventional high explosive (HE) contained in the device.

So why is this important? First a little physics. Nuclear weapons use many different designs to achieve detonation but they all have some characteristics in common. They all fundamentally arrange fissile nuclear materials in a safe, non-critical configuration and then use conventional high explosives (HE) to very quickly and precisely rearrange this fissile material to produce a critical configuration. If anything disturbs the initial design configuration or causes the firing system to operate in anything other than its precisely coordinated and timed sequence, then the needed critical nuclear reaction never occurs even though the explosive force of the HE is fully realized. This creates what may be, for many people, counter intuitive behavior. With conventional explosive weapons, impacting, dropping, or burning of the weapon can be expected to produce full blown detonation for either an individual weapon or, more importantly, a cache of many weapons. This is not the case for nuclear weapons.

For MLD path A, accidental weapon function without command, this means that accidents with nuclear weapons that may be very serious and even include detonation of the HE, but no nuclear yield, do not satisfy our top event.

The actual data on nuclear weapons accidents confirms the above discussion. Using data from the Federation of American Scientists for weapons stockpile histories, we have accumulated approximately two million weapon-years of deployment experience. During that time, accident data published by Wikipedia (Ref 8-1) documents 30 accident events that have put about 62 weapons in some form of severe stress. This includes nine weapons that have experienced accidental HE detonation, all without producing nuclear yield.

So the raw experience data says that we have experienced zero detonations in 2 million weapon-years of deployment. In spite of my above discussion, if we allow a small chance, perhaps one in a thousand, that an unwanted firing could occur during accidental HE ignition, then a point estimate of the likelihood of an accidental weapon detonation for today's global stockpile would be:

$$(9 \div 2E6) \times 0.001 = 4.5E - 9 \frac{detonations}{weaponyear}$$

And for a global stockpile of 4000 deployed weapons, this would sum to about:

$$4.5E - 9 \times 4000 = 1.8E - 5 \; detonations/year$$

In addition to this number being very low, we should also consider that:

- The accidental detonation is for one weapon
- Since nuclear weapons are not typically kept near high population areas, casualties are likely to be low.
- An accidental detonation would probably be recognized as such very quickly by all affected parties, minimizing the likelihood of an escalating incident.

Thus, accidental nuclear weapon detonation does not look like a major source of nuclear war risk.

Chapter 8 References:
8-1.List of military nuclear accidents, *Wikipedia*, 8/27/2017.

Chapter 9 - Nuclear War without Intent

This Chapter examines MLD path B, weapons operated without proper authorization. This branch of the Detonation MLD has been expanded to include a third level. Path B1, spontaneous initiation of firing signal, describes scenarios where even though no firing signal has been given, it is somehow generated and initiates a weapon to function as designed. This is obviously a very serious and unwanted failure mode for a nuclear weapon and has been the focus of considerable attention by weapon builders. To prevent this and other types of possible unwanted weapon detonations, all weapons belonging to the major nuclear powers are equipped with engineered safeguards to prevent unwanted operation. These safeguards are generally known as Permissive Action Links or PALs. To learn what PALs are and how they work to protect against unwanted weapon operation, I would refer you to a quite good article in *Wikipedia* (Ref 9-1). Some of the design features used in PALs include:

- The two-man rule - This prevents the accidental or malicious launch of nuclear weapons by a single individual.
- Stronglinks and Weaklinks – The deliberate design of some weapon components to be fragile and fail safe before their protective housing can be breached.
- Critical signal detection – Design of firing systems to accept only a unique signal that cannot be imitated.
- Environmental recognition – The inclusion of sensors in a weapon that will prevent operation unless they sense that the weapon is in its intended operational environment (e.g. outer space).
- Tamper protection – The inclusion of sensors that will deliberately misfire and destroy the weapon (and all persons nearby) if tampered with.

Collectively, PALs make MLD path B1, spontaneous firing of a weapon, extremely unlikely. This statement may not be true, however, for nuclear weapons built by N Korea or Iran, as we know little or nothing about such weapons.

Launch on false indication of warning or attack

Detonation MLD path B2 includes scenarios where a nation may launch a nuclear attack after receiving a false indication that they have been attacked or are about to be attacked by weapons that have already been launched toward them. The logic that completes this branch of the Nuclear Weapons Detonation MLD is as follows.

Exhibit 9-1 Launch on False Warning Logic

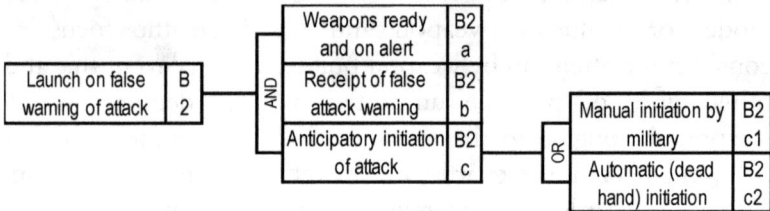

Launch on false warning of attack	B2	AND	Weapons ready and on alert	B2 a			
			Receipt of false attack warning	B2 b	OR	Manual initiation by military	B2 c1
			Anticipatory initiation of attack	B2 c		Automatic (dead hand) initiation	B2 c2

Any of the nuclear weapons states that have weapons on constant alert ready to be launched could be vulnerable to committing a launch on false warning. This scenario is a prime concern for Russia and the U. S. who still believe each other to be capable of a first strike. It is less of a concern for other nuclear weapons states that do not maintain weapons on ready alert. Still, a launch on false warning could be initiated by any nuclear weapons state during a period of heightened tensions.

This category of events is a potentially serious risk contributor as evidenced by several close calls that have occurred in the U.S. and Russian early warning systems. The following exhibit lists the most serious of these events.

Exhibit 9-2 Nuclear False Warning Incidents

Date:	False Indication(s):	Response:
5/1967 (Ref 9-2)	A severe solar storm that raged from May 23 to 27 1967 likely disrupted NORAD sensing and communications systems for an extended period.	The US Air Force Solar Forecasting Unit was able to alert military officials of the storm and its effects to allow compensating measures to be taken and avoid a panic.
11/9/1979 (Ref 9-3)	A training tape at NORAD was mistakenly fed to computers during real time monitoring. All launch centers received an attack alert and began response actions.	Verification checks of raw data feeds by officers on duty indicated no attack was in progress. All alerts were cancelled.
6/3/1980 (Ref 9-3)	A faulty computer chip at NORAD caused a false attack alert to be generated. All launch centers received an attack alert and began response actions.	Verification checks of raw data feeds by officers on duty indicated no attack was in progress. All alerts were cancelled.
9/1983 (Ref 9-3)	A Soviet satellite mistakes reflections from clouds as missile launches	The officer on duty correctly interprets the warning as false.
1/25/1995 (Ref 9-3)	Russian radar falsely reads a Norwegian weather rocket as an attack.	President Yeltsin believes the alarm is false and does not order an attack.

An especially disturbing pathway (B2c2) is one where a nation feels so vulnerable and threatened that it is willing to build a system capable of retaliating to a nuclear attack without human command. Such a Dead Hand or doomsday device has been the subject of much speculation (*Dr. Strangelove*) but the Russian Federation is believed to actually have some type of Dead Hand system that is not normally active but can be turned on in a time of crisis (Ref 9-3). If a doomsday system were to receive a false indication of an attack, unintended war could result.

To prevent a nuclear weapons launch on false warning several things are needed. First, a treaty or other type of mutual agreement is needed that prohibits the construction of Dead Hand systems or doomsday devices, Also sensing and monitoring systems need to be extremely reliable and not give false indications of an attack. Most importantly, there needs to be reliable and trusted communications systems operating among the political and military leaders of all nuclear powers. Since making automatic systems completely foolproof is not possible, reliable and frequently tested direct communications systems are essential to control false warning risk.

To express launch on false warning risk quantitatively, let's look at the three element AND gate in Exhibit 9-1. For now, let's just consider risk from the U.S. and Russia and assume that both nations have weapons on constant alert. Let's also assume that there are no dead hand systems in place. The risk of a launch on false warning then reduces to the frequency of false warnings from the early warning systems times the likelihood of a human failure to recognize the false signal and proceed with weapons launch. Between the U.S. and Russian early warning systems we have something close to 100 years of operating experience. If we then consider the five events listed in Exhibit 9-2 as actual false warning challenges, this gives us a false warning frequency of about 0.05 per year. Based on extensive data, the range of the failure rate that can be credibly given for a practiced but stressful human action is between 0.1 (one error in ten actions) and 0.001 (one error in a thousand actions). So if we pick 0.01 from the middle of this range and multiply this with the false warning frequency estimate, we get a ballpark launch on false warning risk of 0.0005 or 5E-4 per year. We will carry this frequency forward to the MFRA update task and see how significant a risk contributor this might be.

Loss of Command and Control

Pathway B3-B4 includes scenarios where the custody of nuclear weapons is lost to an unauthorized party. This branch does not include scenarios where nuclear weapons are deliberately given to a third party along with their firing codes. Weapons given to a third party knowing they will be used is a first strike attack by proxy and belongs more appropriately to path C3.

For scenarios where the weapons are taken by an unauthorized party, there are two major sub-paths. If weapons are taken by a party that does not have access to the firing code, then they must defeat the PALs described earlier to use the weapons. There is a very low likelihood of this being successful and so the overall risk for this path is low. A secondary risk from weapons theft stems from the possibility that the weapons are not used directly, but the fissile materials are recovered (PALs can't prevent this) and remanufactured to create a useable nuclear weapon. This was the plot for Tom Clancy's *Sum of All Fears*. In that novel, no search for the missing weapon was taken because the original owner could not admit they had it in the first place. It made a good story, but the likelihood of a successful remanufacture is quite low.

The other possibility for unauthorized use of nuclear weapons comes from a scenario where the government possessing the weapons is overthrown and control of the weapons changes to a new party even though the weapons don't actually move. This scenario actually took place during the Russian revolution in 1991. In this case there was no panic and no loss of custody by the Russian military. However, the next time a revolution or coup d'état takes place in a nuclear weapons state, things might unfold differently. If the revolutionary leaders take possession of nuclear weapons and their firing equipment and codes, this could be an extremely dangerous scenario.

Chapter 9 References:

9-1. Permissive Action Links, *Wikipedia*, 9/6/2016.
9-2. *The May 1967 Great Storm and Radio Disruption Event: Extreme Space Weather and Extraordinary Responses*, D. J. Knipp, et al, 2016, American Geophysical Union.
9-3. *False Alarms in the Nuclear Age*, Nova - PBS online, 11/6/2001. http://www.pbs.org/wgbh/nova/military/nuclear-false-alarms.html

9-4. *False Alarms, True Dangers? Current and Future Risks of Inadvertent U.S.-Russian Nuclear War*, Anthony M. Barrett RAND corporation, 2016. http://www.rand.org/pubs/perspectives/PE191.html

Chapter 10 - Nuclear War with Intent

Nuclear Weapons Tests

Path C from the Detonation MLD describes the paths through which nuclear weapons could be used with intent. Path C3 is nuclear weapons testing. Since the Trinity test conducted on July 16, 1945 there have been over 2000 nuclear weapons tests. The frequency of testing remained relatively high through the cold war era, but since then treaty agreements, scientific advances that reduce the need for test data, and reduced tensions have led all nations except North Korea to suspend nuclear weapons tests. The U.S. and Russia continue to perform sub-critical experiments as part of their weapons stewardship programs. Early in the nuclear era these tests were conducted in the atmosphere but by treaty agreement, all nuclear tests conducted since 1980 have been contained underground. Barring some accident in assembling the test device, no one should be harmed by a test and no radiation should be released to the environment. Tests that surprise other nations or that are conducted to intimidate others during a time of heightened tensions could play a role in a larger pattern of aggression. But directly, nuclear tests represent little risk of war.

Retaliation Strikes

MLD path C2 contains scenarios where nuclear weapons are used in retaliation for a confirmed first strike from another party. This does not include an anticipated attack (Path B2) or retaliation for non-nuclear aggression.

There are at least two categories of scenarios feeding into this branch that deserve discussion. The first category is a retaliation responding to a massive first strike. This action amounts to a fulfillment of the mutual assured destruction (MAD) doctrine. It is a strike carried out to insure that an adversary does not survive to benefit from their first use of nuclear weapons. A massive first strike plus a retaliatory strike scenario is also certain to produce global nuclear winter effects.

This scenario is a true Armageddon event but because it is so severe, it may not have a high enough frequency to be a dominant risk contributor.

The second category of events feeding into the C2 branch represents a set of even more troubling scenarios. In this case, a nation has suffered a nuclear attack but it is not an existential massive first strike. Rather, the attack is of a terrorist nature, a limited tactical strike, or the very special case of an indirect EMP attack. I say indirect because an EMP attack may not directly kill anyone although the indirect effects on an urban industrialized population may be devastating. In this type of scenario, the victimized nation must decide how respond. Retaliation could be non-nuclear, nuclear in-kind, or an escalation to a massive nuclear strike. In my assessment, this MLD path may be a significant risk contributor because it represents scenarios where someone may calculate that they could strike an adversary in a limited way and not provoke a nuclear response. If the calculation turns out to be wrong, then we have Armageddon.

As we focus on risk, however, we have to keep in mind that whether or not a retaliation strike occurs affects only the consequences of nuclear war, not the frequency. If there is no first strike, there can be no retaliation strike.

First Strikes

MLD path C1 represents scenarios where a nation deliberately chooses to use nuclear weapons under its command and control against an adversary. Since there can be no expectation of surviving a nuclear exchange, the use of these weapons must be the result of a calculation (or miscalculation) that no nuclear winter effect will occur from the first strike and that there will be no retaliatory strike. To engage in the first use of nuclear weapons expecting retaliation and a nuclear winter is madness. You may react to this statement by thinking that any use of nuclear weapons is by definition madness since the calculation window I describe does not really exist. For sure, to even consider the use of nuclear weapons, a nation would have to suffer some event or events that place them in a perceived state of existential crisis. How could this possibly happen? Let's begin by reviewing what the nuclear armed nations themselves have formally said about the use nuclear weapons. The following exhibit provides a short description of each nation's formal policy for the use of nuclear weapons.

Exhibit 10-1 Nuclear First Use Policies

Country	First Use Policy
Russia	Russia reserves the right to use nuclear weapons in response to the use of nuclear and other types of weapons of mass destruction against it or its allies, and also in case of aggression against Russia with the use of conventional weapons when the very existence of the state is threatened.
United States	The United States would only consider the use of nuclear weapons in extreme circumstances to defend the vital interests of the United States or its allies and partners.
France	"French nuclear deterrence is the ultimate guarantee of our sovereignty" and "protects France from any State-led aggression against its vital interests, of whatever origin and in whatever form. It rules out any threat of blackmail that might paralyze its freedom of decision and action".
China	China will not be the first to use nuclear weapons at any time or under any circumstances.
United Kingdom	The UK has long been clear that we would only consider using our nuclear weapons in extreme circumstances of self defense, including the defense of our NATO Allies, and we remain deliberately ambiguous about precisely when, how and at what scale we would contemplate their use
Israel	Israel has no nuclear use policy since it does not admit to having nuclear weapons. However, it is widely believed that it would attempt a retaliation attack should the State of Israel be seriously jeopardized.
Pakistan	Pakistan has vowed never to invade or attack another country under any circumstances, although if ever invaded or attacked, it will use "any weapon in its arsenal" to defend itself.
India	India will not be the first to initiate a nuclear first strike, but will respond with punitive retaliation should deterrence fail.
North Korea	North Korea would not use nuclear weapons first unless aggressive hostile forces use nuclear weapons to invade on our sovereignty.
Iran	Iranian leaders have repeatedly stated that Iran has no intention of developing nuclear weapons and thus has no need for a nuclear use policy.

The above criteria for nuclear weapon use can be generally captured in two phrases *"self defense"* and *"vital interests"*. "Self defense" may seem straightforward but quite little definition is given for "vital interests". Notably, the Brits even state that they will "remain deliberately ambiguous" about what they are. Understanding is further complicated by the extension of vital interests to include allies. After reading several long discussions of this subject, I constructed the following concise list of what I think captures the most vital of interests that all nations share. These are:

1. Homeland security free from assault or the threat of assault from other states or terrorist organizations.

2. Political independence free of external interference

3. Freedom and security of travel through open waters, open skies, and outer space.

4. Fair trade access to needed materials and goods

5. Access to a secure and stable international monetary and financial system

Furthermore, I interpret alliances between two nations to mean that they commit to defend these vital interests on behalf of each other. In addition, most nuclear weapons states have other nations beyond committed allies that they consider to be within their "sphere of influence". Whether or not they would provide military assistance to such states in a time of crisis will be a critical question in determining war and peace.

If taken at face value, the stated first use policies leave us with a sense of good will. No nations harbor hostilities against others and would only use nuclear weapons in extreme circumstances of self-defense. So what's the problem? Simply put, there is at least one glaring omission to the stated first use policies, the aggression shield.

The governments of the nuclear weapons states can be divided into two reasonably clear groups, the democracies and the autocracies. Nine of the ten nuclear weapons states are easily categorized. I'll count Pakistan as a democracy even though it has struggled to stay that way, having spent 33 of its 70 years under military rule. This then gives us a total of six democracies and four autocracies.

Many scholars of history, economics and political science have noted that autocracies are much more likely to initiate conflicts with other nations and conduct democides against their own people than are democracies. This behavior is generally called "democratic peace" and I invite you to research it on your own if you doubt the validity of this proposition. In contrast to democratic peace, autocracies endorse violence against anyone internal or external that does not embrace the particular ideology of their ruler. The importance of this behavior to our discussion here is that, for an autocracy, an unwritten justification for at least the threat of nuclear weapons first use is to shield any hostile actions deemed necessary to defend and spread its ideology. This belief that aggression is justified to spread ideology causes autocracies to identify targets that they believe are incompatible with their beliefs for aggression. The war data in Chapter 2 shows that before nuclear weapons, autocracies often acted on these hostile intentions. But in the aftermath of WWII the United States, acting with its allies, extended its nuclear deterrent shield over many other nations to break this cycle of violence and prevent the wider proliferation of nuclear weapons.

In addition to the extended deterrent shield, the United States and its WWII allies have assumed an even wider array of international responsibilities. Although all nations would consider the vital interests #3, 4, & 5 to be important to their own viability, it has become the defacto global responsibility of the U.S. Navy to guarantee freedom of the seas, the U.S. Air Force to guarantee freedom of the skies, and the U.S. Government to guarantee the stability and integrity of the World Bank, International Monetary Fund, World Trade Organization, and United Nations. With respect to the United Nations, all nuclear powers have a degree of vital interest in supporting the agencies that monitor and enforce treaties banning the spread of weapons of mass destruction. These include the International Atomic Energy Agency, the Chemical

Weapons Convention, and the Biological Weapons Convention. The net result of the U.S. taking on these added responsibilities is that the vital interests of United States can be attacked indirectly by undermining any of these responsibilities or institutions.

Taking the aggression and deterrence shield criteria into account with the other vital interests, we can now construct a map that represents the current state of the vital interests of the nuclear weapons states. First, let's consider the relationships among the nuclear weapons states. As you might infer from the discussion above, the nuclear weapons states with autocratic governments are generally aligned in opposition to those with democratic governments. As of this writing (summer 2017), the vital interests and spheres of influence of each nuclear power are reasonably well understood and respected. In other words, a general equilibrium exists among the nuclear weapons states.

One other bi-lateral nuclear relationship deserves special mention. India and Pakistan are neighbors that shared a common history up to 1947 and because of differences rooted in the Hindu and Muslim religions that shape their cultures and governments, have been in a constant state of conflict ever since separation. The development of nuclear weapons by India (1974) and Pakistan (1998) occurred without clear aid from other nuclear nations, and they continue to be formally unaligned with either the autocratic or democratic weapons states. So far they have both followed a no first use policy for nuclear weapons use, but recent reports indicate that this could soon change and escalate their level of mutual hostility to a new more dangerous level (Ref 10-1)

Now let's look at the role alliances play in this game. For this part of our analysis, I have included Israel and Iran in their official non-nuclear status since an official change in their nuclear status would disturb the equilibrium.

Exhibit 10-2 Nuclear Aggression & Deterrence

	USA	UK	France	Pakistan	India	Russia	China	N Korea
Country								
NATO: Non-Nuclear	CP	CP	CP			T		
Sweden	SA	SA	SA			T		
Belarus						CP		
Ukraine	SA	SA	SA			V		
Georgia						V		
Egypt								
Saudi Arabia	SA	SA	SA					
Yemen								
Israel	CP	SA	SA					
Iraq	CP	SA	SA					
Iran						SA	SA	SA
Syria	V	V	V			CP		
Libya	SA	SA	SA			T		
Afghanistan	CP	SA		SA		T		
Japan	CP	SA				T	T	T
South Korea	CP					T	T	T
Taiwan	SA						T	T
Philippines							T	
Vietnam							T	
Australia	CP	CP	SA				T	
Indonesia								
Canada	CP	CP	SA			T		
Cuba	T					SA		

The columns are grouped under the header **Nuclear Weapon States**. The row axis is labeled **Perception of Relationship with Nuclear Weapons States**.

T - Target of aggression from
V - Victim of aggression by
CP - Committed protector
SA - Supportive ally

The pattern that emerges from this exhibit is one where the inherent tendency of the autocracies for aggression is balanced by the deterrent shield of the United States and its allies. I again propose that the above security conditions represent, without judgement, a geopolitical equilibrium condition that all parties have some interest in maintaining. The autocracies need enemies, but they do not need actual war. This situation resembles what game theory calls a "Nash Equilibrium". A Nash Equilibrium is a stable state in which no participant can gain an advantage in the game by a unilateral change of strategy if the strategies of the other players remain the same. The first use of nuclear weapons will then require a departure from the equilibrium condition that results in the violation of the vital interests of at least one nuclear weapons state.

Chapter 10 References:

10-1. India, Pakistan Escalate Nuclear Race, Saeed Shah, *The Wall Street Journal*, 4/1-2/2017.

Chapter 11 - Survival Games

We have now reduced the question of how a nuclear first strike with intent could occur to the outcome of a deadly game. The initial conditions are set as described in the previous chapter. If the equilibrium condition among the nuclear weapons states is disturbed, there are two possible outcomes: the acceptance by all players of a new equilibrium or war. Deal the cards.

Once again I will use a master logic diagram (MLD) to chart the possible pathways of events that could produce a nuclear first strike decision. The MLD that follows below is an extension of path C1 from Exhibit 7-1.

Exhibit 11-1 MLD for First Strike Decision

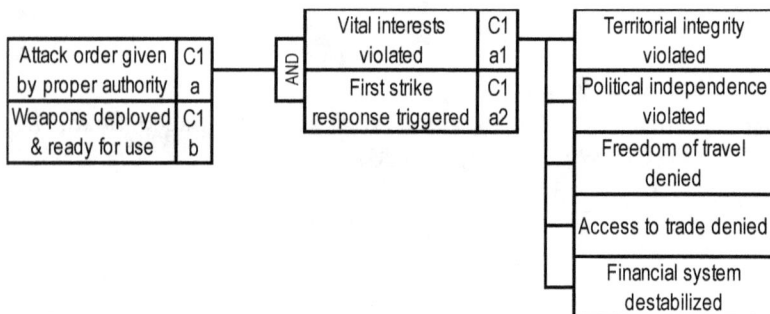

Attack order given	C1	AND	Vital interests violated	C1 a1		Territorial integrity violated
by proper authority	a		First strike response triggered	C1 a2		Political independence violated
Weapons deployed	C1					Freedom of travel denied
& ready for use	b					Access to trade denied
						Financial system destabilized

This MLD shows that a first strike attack order requires the satisfaction of an AND gate with two branches. First, there must be a destabilizing event that disturbs the current equilibrium among the nuclear weapons states and violates the vital interests of at least one state (path C1a1). Plus, the violated state or states must refuse to accept the new equilibrium condition that would result from the destabilizing event and rationalize that a nuclear first strike is their only or best option (path C1a2). In other words, a nuclear first strike order will emanate from a decision that capitulation to whatever violation of perceived vital interests has occurred cannot or will not be tolerated.

There are at least two possible categories of rationalization that allow this. The first category would come from a nation that feels that its vital interests have been violated by a superior foe and is fearful that their forces will be destroyed by a tactical nuclear or conventional first strike from the superior foe. As a result, they elect to strike first as an act of desperation and perhaps stave off an even larger attack by the initially superior foe. The second category of attack rationalization allows for the calculation that the risk of retaliation may be acceptably low. This could be because the potential target of the attack may not possess nuclear weapons. Or, any nuclear weapons the target may have could be destroyed by the first strike. And finally, the target state may be intimidated from retaliation by the threat of a second attack. I didn't say they were good rationalizations. Ominously, these two rationalizations can work simultaneously to create a very dangerous situation whenever a confrontation occurs between a very capable nuclear weapons state and a much less capable nuclear weapons state.

But since our objective here is the assessment of risk, we need a systematic framework for estimating the likelihood that these conditions have been satisfied. At this point it is easy to see that the logic behind a first strike decision will be complicated and perhaps not entirely rational. The formation of such a dramatic decision will likely be the product of a long escalation scenario that will have, from the decision maker's point of view, many off ramps where the adversary or adversaries could have accommodated their vital interests without war. In other words, before a first strike decision is reached, measurable tensions will rise from normal equilibrium levels. This increasing tension will likely be proportional to the severity of the disequilibrium event from path C1a1. So how can we hope to make an assessment of this behavior that is practical and useful? I think I have pressed the top-down or deductive approach to the first strike question as far as is useful. Now it is time to identify specific situations that could produce war and screen them for importance.

To accomplish this screening process I chose to use a qualitative risk ranking method similar to those described in *Risk Management Revisited*. The task of assessing first strike risk requires that we examine the geopolitical situations where confrontations between nuclear armed states could spin out of control and lead to nuclear war. I'll call these situations *conflict theaters*. To limit the complexity of the task, we will only examine conflict theaters where two nuclear armed states are in adversarial positions. In each conflict theater we will evaluate the potential first strike risk presented by each adversary. The list of conflict theaters and adversaries we will examine is as follows.

Exhibit 11-2 Conflict Theaters & Adversaries

Conflict Theater	Risk of First Strike from
Kashmir	India1
	Pakistan
Sikkim	India2
	China1
Korea	N Korea
	USA1
S China Sea	China2
	USA2
Ukraine	Russia1
	NATO/USA3
Baltics/ E Europe	Russia2
	NATO/USA4
Syria/Iraq	Russia3
	NATO/USA5
Israel	Iran
	Israel
Crashwar	China3
	USA6

You will note that all the conflict theaters are defined by traditional territorial disputes except for the last one. Crashwar represents a nuclear war stemming from an economic rather that a territorial dispute. China is now the world's second largest economy, is a full participant in the U.S. led global financial system, and holds over three trillion dollars' worth of U.S. treasury bonds. Thus, the Chinese government has the capability to wage economic war as well as nuclear war with the U.S. and the other democratic nuclear weapons states. Russia, Iran, and N Korea lack this economic power.

I then structured the first strike risk analysis by defining two risk metrics, conflict initiation risk and escalation to nuclear weapons risk. For each of these risk metrics I identified risk factors for which I developed qualitative ranking scales that I could apply to each nuclear weapons state in each conflict theater. I then combined the rakings for conflict risk and escalation risk in a risk matrix format to present final qualitative rankings for each country in each conflict theater. Later, I will use these qualitative rankings (high, medium, low) to estimate quantitative ranges for the likelihood of nuclear conflict. The next three exhibits illustrate the qualitative risk ranking process and present the risk factors and qualitative scales that will be used in the risk ranking.

Exhibit 11-3 Nuclear First Strike Risk Ranking Process

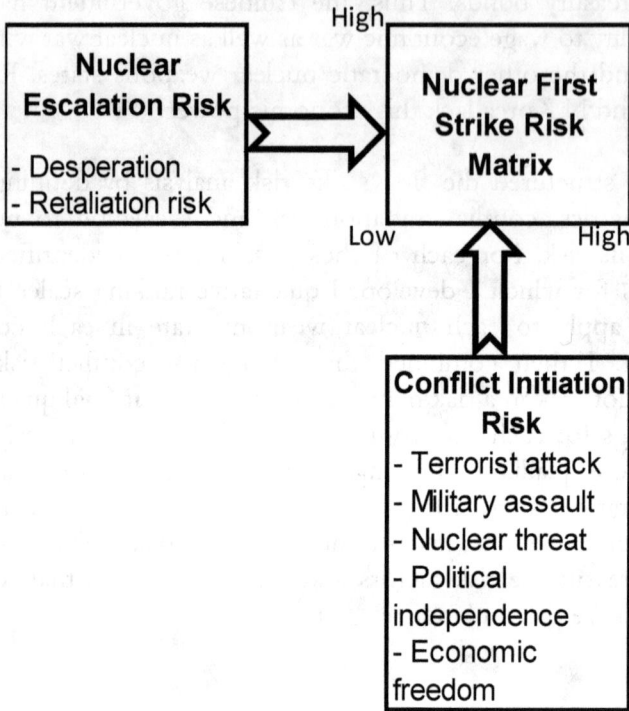

	High	
Nuclear Escalation Risk - Desperation - Retaliation risk	⟹	**Nuclear First Strike Risk Matrix**
	Low High	

Conflict Initiation Risk
- Terrorist attack
- Military assault
- Nuclear threat
- Political independence
- Economic freedom

Exhibit 11-4 Conflict Initiation Risk Factors

Terrorist assault risk	The adversary is cooperating in a meaningful way with others to control terrorism. No sanctuary or assistance is being given to terrorist groups.	The adversary is inconsistent in cooperating with others to control terrorism. Covert sanctuary or assistance may being given to terrorist groups.	The adversary is not cooperating in a meaningful way with others to control terrorism. Overt sanctuary or assistance is being given to terrorist groups.
Conventional military assault risk	The adversary has threatened to use conventional military force against this nation or its vital interests.	The adversary has assembled conventional military forces in a position that potentially threatens this nation or its vital interests.	The adversary has taken confrontational military actions that threaten this nation or its vital interests.
Nuclear assault risk	The adversary maintains a no first use policy for nuclear weapons use.	The adversary has not established a no first use policy for nuclear weapons use, but has issued no explicit threats of nuclear weapons use against this government.	The adversary has issued explicit first use threats of nuclear weapons use against this government.
Political integrity risk	The adversary respects the legitimacy and independence of this nation. Mutual participation in international organizations is serving to limit conflict.	The adversary acknowledges the legitimacy and independence of this nation, but cooperation has been replaced by disinformation and obstruction in international organizations.	The adversary does not recognize the legitimacy of this government and is openly advocating regime change.
Economic freedom risk	The adversary has taken no action to affect the ability of this nation to travel or trade freely, or to access international financial systems.	The adversary has enacted economic sanctions that are intended to influence the behavior of this government.	The adversary has enacted economic sanctions that are intended to disrupt the ability of this government to function.

Exhibit 11-5 Nuclear Escalation Risk Factors

Risk Factor	Risk Ranking Scale		
	Low (1)	Medium (3)	High (5)
Desperation	The political, economic, and military powers of this nation and/or its allies are substantial and provide multiple means for responding to any violation of vital interests, escalation to nuclear conflict is low.	The political, economic, and military powers of this nation to respond to a violation of vital interests are limited or its allies are not completely committed to its defense, the risk of escalation to nuclear conflict is significant.	The political, economic, and military powers of this nation to respond to a violation of vital interests are limited and it has no allies committed to its defense, the risk of escalation to nuclear conflict is high.
Retaliation Risk	The adversary facing this nation has robust and diverse nuclear weapons capabilities or a committed and reliable ally. Nuclear retaliation to a first strike is certain, therefore the risk of a first strike being initiated low.	The adversary facing this nation has little or no nuclear weapons capabilities but does have a nuclear capable ally. However the reliability of this ally to provide a first strike response is uncertain, making retaliation risk unknown.	The adversary facing this nation has little or no nuclear weapons capabilities and no committed allies to provide deterrence. This makes the risk of retaliation to a first strike low and the risk of a first strike being initiated high.

The definitions of the risk factors and risk rankings for each country in each conflict theater are based solely on my judgement as documented above. The combined conflict and escalation risk rankings are intended to represent the risk of conflict occurring and escalating to nuclear war under the current geopolitical environment.

The exhibits that follow present the risk ranking worksheets for each conflict theater. The numeric risk rankings (1 to 5) for each country in each conflict theater are based solely on my judgement as documented in the worksheets. The presentation and discussion of the first strike risk results follow the worksheets.

Exhibit 11-6 First Strike Risk Ranking Worksheets

Conflict Theater:	South Asia
Adversaries:	1) India
	2) Pakistan

Conflict Risk Ranking			
	Attack by:		
Risk Factor	India	Pakistan	Comments
Terrorist assault risk	4.5	2.0	Pakistani terrorist stage attacks in both countries
Conventional military	4.0	4.0	Military clashes occur often in Kashmir
Nuclear assault risk	2.0	1.0	
Political integrity risk	2.0	2.0	
Economic freedom risk	2.5	2.5	Little if any direct trade
Conflict Initiation Risk	4.5	4.0	

Escalation Risk Ranking			
	Attack by:		
Risk Factor	India	Pakistan	Comments
Desperation	1.0	2.0	
Retaliation Risk	2.0	2.0	
Escalation Risk Ranking	2.0	2.0	
First Strike Risk Ranking	3.3	3.0	

Survival Games

Conflict Theater:	Korea
Adversaries:	1) North Korea
	2) South Korea/USA

Conflict Risk Ranking			
Risk Factor	Attack by:		Comments
	N Korea	USA	
Terrorist assault risk	1.0	4.0	Terrorist type attacks by the N are possible
Conventional military	3.0	4.0	
Nuclear assault risk	3.0	4.0	NK's threats exceed its capability, for now
Political integrity risk	4.5	4.0	U.S. long term goal is a unified Korea
Economic freedom risk	1.0	4.0	
Conflict Initiation Risk	4.5	4.0	

Escalation Risk Ranking			
Risk Factor	Attack by:		Comments
	N Korea	USA	
Desperation	2.5	0.0	
Retaliation Risk	1.0	2.5	A preemptive US strike may be the highest risk
Escalation Risk Ranking	2.5	2.5	
First Strike Risk Ranking	3.5	3.3	

Survival Games

Conflict Theater:	South China Sea
Adversaries:	1) China
	2) USA2

Conflict Risk Ranking			
	Attack by:		
Risk Factor	China	USA2	Comments
Terrorist assault risk	1.0	1.0	
Conventional military	3.5	3.0	China's hostility to all parties seems irrational.
Nuclear assault risk	1.0	1.0	
Political integrity risk	2.0	1.0	
Economic freedom risk	1.0	1.0	
Conflict Initiation Risk	3.5	3.0	

Escalation Risk Ranking			
	Attack by:		
Risk Factor	China	USA2	Comments
Desperation	0.0	0.0	
Retaliation Risk	1.0	1.0	
Escalation Risk Ranking	1.0	1.0	
First Strike Risk Ranking	2.3	2.0	

Conflict Theater:	Ukraine
Adversaries:	1) Russia1
	2) USA3

Conflict Risk Ranking			
	Attack by:		
Risk Factor	**Russia1**	**USA3**	**Comments**
Terrorist assault risk	1.0	2.0	
Conventional military	2.0	3.0	
Nuclear assault risk	1.0	2.0	
Political integrity risk	2.0	3.0	
Economic freedom risk	3.0	1.0	
Conflict Initiation Risk Ranking	3.0	3.0	Appeasement of Russia is likely to invite further aggression

Escalation Risk Ranking			
	Attack by:		
Risk Factor	**Russia**	**USA3**	**Comments**
Desperation	0.0	0.0	
Retaliation Risk	1.0	1.3	
Escalation Risk Ranking	1.0	1.3	
First Strike Risk Ranking	2.0	2.1	

Conflict Theater:	Baltics/East Europe
Adversaries:	1) Russia2
	2) USA4

Conflict Risk Ranking			
	Attack by:		
Risk Factor	Russia2	USA4	Comments
Terrorist assault risk	1.0	2.0	
Conventional military	3.2	3.0	Russia feels threatened by Baltics joining NATO
Nuclear assault risk	2.0	2.0	
Political integrity risk	1.0	2.0	Russia feels threatened by Baltics joining NATO
Economic freedom risk	1.0	1.0	
Conflict Initiation Risk	3.2	3.0	

Escalation Risk Ranking			
	Attack by:		
Risk Factor	Russia2	USA4	Comments
Desperation	0.0	0.0	
Retaliation Risk	1.0	1.6	
Escalation Risk Ranking	1.0	1.6	
First Strike Risk Ranking	2.1	2.3	

Conflict Theater:	Syria & Iraq
Adversaries:	1) Russia3
	2) USA5

Conflict Risk Ranking			
	Attack by:		
Risk Factor	Russia3	USA5	Comments
Terrorist assault risk	1.5	1.5	
Conventional military assault risk	4.1	4.2	Incidents between US & Russian forces could escalate
Nuclear assault risk	2.0	2.0	
Political integrity risk	3.0	3.0	
Economic freedom risk	1.0	1.0	
Conflict Initiation Risk	4.1	4.2	

Escalation Risk Ranking			
	Attack by:		
Risk Factor	Russia3	USA5	Comments
Desperation	0.0	0.0	
Retaliation Risk	1.0	1.0	
Escalation Risk Ranking	1.0	1.0	
First Strike Risk Ranking	2.6	2.6	

Conflict Theater:	Israel
Adversaries:	1) Iran
	2) Israel/USA6

Conflict Risk Ranking			
	Attack by:		
Risk Factor	Iran	Israel	Comments
Terrorist assault risk	2.0	4.5	Terrorist attacks in Israel could rise to open war
Conventional military	3.0	4.3	Iranian & US/Israeli forces could clash in Syria
Nuclear assault risk	1.5	1.0	
Political integrity risk	3.0	4.5	Iran routinely threatens to destroy Israel
Economic freedom risk	3.0	1.0	
Conflict Initiation Risk	3.0	4.5	

Escalation Risk Ranking			
	Attack by:		
Risk Factor	Iran	Israel	Comments
Desperation	1.5	0.0	US deterrent forces are adequate to prevent escalation for now.
Retaliation Risk	1.0	1.0	
Escalation Risk Ranking	1.5	1.0	
First Strike Risk Ranking	2.3	2.8	

Conflict Theater:	Crashwar
Adversaries:	1) China3
	2) USA6

Conflict Risk Ranking			
	Attack by:		
Risk Factor	China3	USA6	Comments
Terrorist assault risk	1.0	1.0	
Conventional military	3.0	3.0	
Nuclear assault risk	1.0	1.0	
Political integrity risk	2.0	1.0	
Economic freedom risk	3.0	3.5	The Chinese economic agression could cause a crash in the U.S.
Conflict Initiation Risk	3.0	3.5	

Escalation Risk Ranking			
	Attack by:		
Risk Factor	China3	USA6	Comments
Desperation	2.0	2.0	
Retaliation Risk	1.0	1.0	
Escalation Risk Ranking	2.0	2.0	
First Strike Risk Ranking	2.5	2.8	

Exhibit 11-7 Nuclear First Strike Risk Ranking Results

Conflict Theater	Risk of First Strike from	Conflict Risk	Escalation Risk	First Strike Risk
Kashmir	India1	4.50	2.00	3.25
	Pakistan	4.00	2.00	3.00
Sikkim	India2	4.00	3.00	3.50
	China1	4.50	2.00	3.25
Korea	N Korea	4.50	2.50	3.50
	USA1	4.00	2.50	3.25
S China Sea	China2	3.50	1.00	2.25
	USA2	3.00	1.00	2.00
Ukraine	Russia1	3.00	1.00	2.00
	NATO/USA3	3.00	1.25	2.13
Baltics/ E Europe	Russia2	3.20	1.00	2.10
	NATO/USA4	3.00	1.60	2.30
Syria/Iraq	Russia3	4.10	1.00	2.55
	NATO/USA5	4.20	1.00	2.60
Israel	Iran	3.00	1.50	2.25
	Israel	4.50	1.00	2.75
Crashwar	China3	3.00	2.50	2.75
	USA6	3.50	2.75	3.13
Risk ranking scale:		Low (1)	Medium (2)	High (5)

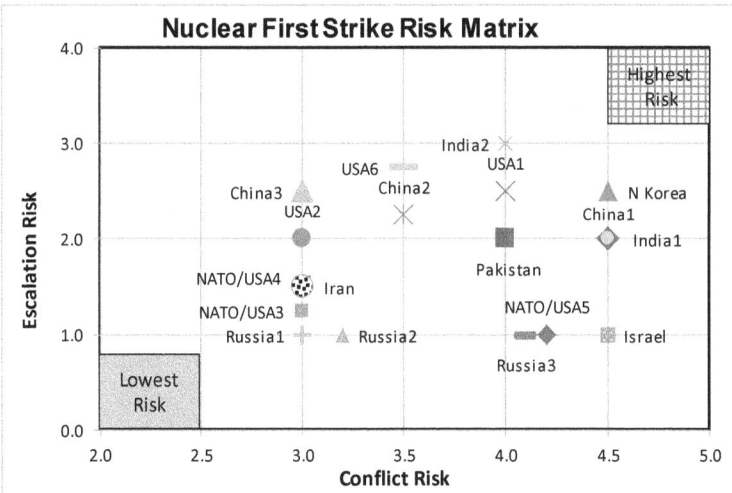

Nuclear First Strike Risk Matrix

The combined first strike risk scores were obtained by averaging the conflict and escalation risk rankings. This method was used because both conflict and escalation are required to produce nuclear war. The results of this qualitative assessment indicate that the risk of nuclear conflict is low or medium for all conflict theaters. The highest risk ranking for a nuclear first strike went to North Korea. India in South Asia and the USA in Korea received the next highest rankings.

To be useful in updating the MFRA, we will need to make a quantitative interpretation of these qualitative analysis results. Since we have recorded 72 years of coexistence now without nuclear war and have previously described the current state of geopolitical relations as being stable, the evidence indicates that the annual frequency for nuclear conflict should be assessed quantitatively in the range of 5E-3 per year or less across all conflict theaters (Ref 107). This would require the frequency for each individual nation in each conflict theater to be in the range of (5E-3/16) or about 3E-4 per year. From this anchor point, we can then use the qualitative risk ranking results to bias the frequencies up or down in proportion with the risk rankings. The following exhibit presents this frequency interpretation.

Exhibit 11-8 Frequency Ranges for First Strike Risk

Qualitative Risk Rank	Frequency Range		
	min	best estimate	max
Low	1.0E-05	3.0E-05	5.0E-05
Medium	1.0E-04	3.0E-04	5.0E-04
High	1.0E-03	3.0E-03	5.0E-03

We will carry these frequencies forward to the MFRA update task and see how significant a risk contributor they might be.

There are at least two significant sources of uncertainty in these risk rankings. First is my obviously imperfect state of knowledge regarding the real intentions of the nuclear weapons states being evaluated. This source of uncertainty is addressed by allowing the estimated first strike frequencies to be represented by broad distributions.

The second and I think more significant source of uncertainty comes from the possibility that the current stable state of geopolitical relations among the nuclear weapons states could change. Anything that disturbs the geopolitical equilibrium among the nuclear weapons states could significantly change the risk rankings we would assign for both conflict and escalation risk.

In the next chapter we will attempt to put some definition to the risk of instability within the nuclear weapons states.

Chapter 12 - Nuclear Weapons State Instability

For our purpose here, instability in a nuclear weapons state is the risk that a state alters its behavior sufficiently to cause the conflict initiation and/or escalation risks assigned in the last chapter to change. This change in behavior may or may not be accompanied by a formal announcement of a revision in vital interests. Because we have described the current state of geopolitical relations among the nuclear weapons states to be a type of Nash Equilibrium, a significant change in behavior by one nuclear power should be expected to provoke behavioral changes by other states in response until a new equilibrium is established.

All potential changes in nuclear weapons state stability are not equal, however. An increase in aggression posture by an autocratic state will cause uncertainty to grow in the first strike risk metrics. A decrease in aggression posture by an autocratic state is also straightforward to assess but the risk of war will decrease or even disappear. This is because the U.S. deterrence shield does not automatically expand to fill the void created by a shrinking aggression posture, making any chance of war less likely. We actually had the chance to observe this type of change when the Soviet Union collapsed in 1991 and no global crisis ensued.

There is one potential geopolitical change, however, that could be very destabilizing. If the U.S. deterrence shield should drop without an adequate replacement, then the aggression postures of the autocratic states at multiple conflict points would expand and attempt to fill the resulting void. But this process would be fraught with uncertainty, greatly increasing the likelihood of war. Thus, the stability of all nuclear weapons states is important but the stability of the United States is truly critical to global peace.

To assess state instability I first looked for work already done by others that I could use. The World Bank, IMF, and others already rank the stability of nations from a perspective that meets their needs. But I didn't find that any of these rankings done by others really focused on the risk factors that could cause the likelihood of nuclear war to change, so I crafted my own system. To do this I selected two risk metrics, political instability risk and economic instability risk. For each of these risk metrics I defined risk factors for which I developed qualitative ranking scales that I could apply to each nuclear weapons state and assess political and economic instability risk separately. I then combined the rankings for the two risk metrics in a risk matrix format to present final qualitative rankings for each country. These qualitative rankings (high, medium, low) can then be used to conditionally change the probabilities for nuclear conflict calculated in the last chapter. The qualitative risk ranking process is illustrated in the next exhibit and the instability risk assessment results and worksheets are presented on the pages that follow.

Exhibit 12-1 State Instability Risk Ranking Process

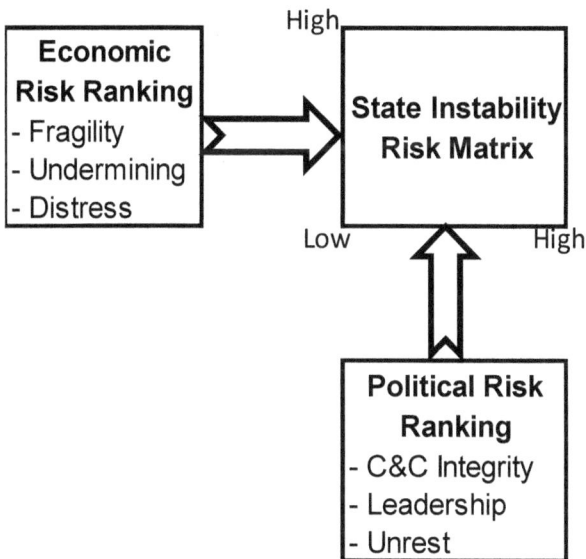

Again in this analysis, the definitions of the risk metrics and risk rankings (1 to 5) for each country are based solely on my judgement and experience in performing qualitative risk analyses. The instability risk rankings are intended to represent the risk of instability occurring during the decade or so from now to the year 2030. The exhibits that follow present the worksheets for each instability risk metric and the weighted results for political and economic instability as well as the combined state instability rankings.

Exhibit 12-2 Political Instability Risk Rankings

Nuclear Weapons State	Total Weighted Risk Score 100%	Risk Factors		
		Command & Control Integrity 40%	Leadership Rationality 40%	Social Unrest 20%
Russia	2.60	2.0	3.5	2.0
United States	2.00	1.0	2.5	3.0
France	1.30	1.0	1.0	2.5
China	2.20	2.0	2.5	2.0
United Kingdom	1.60	1.0	2.0	2.0
Israel	1.20	1.0	1.0	2.0
Pakistan	3.40	3.5	3.5	3.0
India	2.20	2.0	2.5	2.0
North Korea	3.70	3.0	4.5	3.5
Iran	3.50	3.0	4.0	3.5

Risk ranking scale

Low (1)	Medium (3)	High (5)

86

Survival Games

COMMAND & CONTROL INTEGRITY RISK FACTOR

DESCRIPTION	DISCUSSION
Nuclear weapons command and control integrity risk	This is a measure of the stability of a nations command authority for nuclear weapons and the security of the systems used to authorize nuclear weapons use.

RANKING SCALE

LOW (1)	MEDIUM (3)	HIGH (5)
Decision making responsibility is clearly identified and stable. Control systems have been demonstrated to be reliable.	Decision making responsibility is not fully known but is believed to be stable. Control systems are not fully understood but no reliability issues have been observed.	This nation has experienced unconstitutional leadership changes that could threaten weapons command & control.

RISK RANKING

Nuclear Weapons State	Risk Score	Trend (+/- 0.5)	Risk Rank	Comments
Russia	2.0	O	2.0	
USA	1.0	O	1.0	
France	1.0	O	1.0	
China	2.0	O	2.0	
UK	1.0	O	1.0	
Israel	1.0	O	1.0	
Pakistan	3.5	+	4.0	
India	2.0	O	2.0	
N Korea	3.0	O	3.0	
Iran	3.0	O	3.0	

Survival Games

LEADERSHIP RATIONALITY RISK FACTOR

DESCRIPTION	DISCUSSION
Leadership Rationality	This is a measure of the clarity with which a nations vital interests are specified and communicated to allies and adversaries

RANKING SCALE

LOW (1)	MEDIUM (3)	HIGH (5)
Vital interests are limited in scope, rational, and well know by allies and adversaries.	Vital interests are generally well known and rational, but specifics may be deliberately vague.	Vital interests are vague, changeable, and even irrational.

RISK RANKING

Nuclear Weapons State	Risk Score	Trend (+/- 0.5)	Risk Rank	Comments
Russia	3.5	-	3.0	Recent political leadership has been consistently more aggressive. Future Russian aggression posture after Putin is a wild card.
USA	2.5	+	3.0	Deterrence vital interests are extensive, incorporating almost all conflict areas. Recent political leadership has been somewhat inconsistent.
France	1.0	O	1.0	
China	2.5	-	2.0	Recent political leadership has been somewhat more aggressive.
UK	2.0	O	2.0	
Israel	1.0	O	1.0	
Pakistan	3.5	O	3.5	Pakistan has a history of supporting proliferation.
India	2.5	-	2.0	Political leadership has threatened to drop its no first use policy.
N Korea	4.5	-	4.0	Recent political leadership has been consistently more aggressive.
Iran	4.0	O	4.0	Nuclear weapons capability is likely to be revealed within the next decade

Survival Games

SOCIAL UNREST RISK FACTOR

DESCRIPTION	DISCUSSION
Social Unrest	This risk measures the likelihood that internal violence, civil disobedience, or challenges to the legitimacy of authority could force changes in vital interests and aggression or deterrence postures.

RANKING SCALE

LOW (1)	MEDIUM (3)	HIGH (5)
The social stress level is low with no significant dissent to government policies and actions.	The social stress level is visible but civil institutions appear capable of maintaining civil order.	The social stress level is high with the ability of civil institutions to maintain civil order in question. Or, civil order appears outwardly calm but only because of military repression.

RISK RANKING

Nuclear Weapons State	Risk Score	Trend (+/- 0.5)	Risk Rank	Comments
Russia	2.0	O	2.0	Satisfaction with the Putin regime seems high.
USA	3.0	-	2.5	The refusal of radical socialists to acknowledge the legitimacy of President Trump could lead to violence.
France	2.5	O	2.5	Terrorist attacks have created unrest but a presidential election has just been completed peacefully.
China	2.0	O	2.0	
UK	2.0	O	2.0	
Israel	2.0	O	2.0	
Pakistan	3.0	O	3.0	
India	2.0	O	2.0	
N Korea	3.5	O	3.5	Repression conceals any possible sign of unrest.
Iran	3.5	O	3.5	Repression conceals any possible sign of unrest.

Exhibit 12-3 Economic Instability Risk Rankings

Nuclear Weapons State	Total Weighted Risk Score 100%	Risk Factors		
		Economic Fragility 20%	Strategic Undermining 60%	Economic Distress 20%
Russia	1.90	1.5	2.0	2.0
United States	4.10	4.0	5.0	1.5
France	3.70	3.0	4.0	3.5
China	2.50	2.0	2.5	3.0
United Kingdom	3.80	3.5	4.5	2.0
Israel	2.00	2.0	2.0	2.0
Pakistan	2.40	3.0	2.0	3.0
India	1.90	2.0	2.0	1.5
North Korea	1.50	4.5	0.0	3.0
Iran	1.40	2.0	1.0	2.0

Risk ranking scale

Low (1)	Medium (3)	High (5)

Survival Games

ECONOMIC FRAGILITY RISK FACTOR

DESCRIPTION	DISCUSSION
Economic fragility risk	This is a measure of the risk that a national economy is vulnerable to an external event that triggers an economic crisis and forces changes in vital interests and aggression or deterrence postures.

RANKING SCALE

LOW (1)	MEDIUM (3)	HIGH (5)
This nation's economy is diverse and robust and government financial reserves are adequate to address a wide scope of adverse events.	This nation's economy is generally diverse and robust but government financial reserves may not be adequate to address an adverse external event.	This nation's economy is significantly dependent on a single product that is subject to severe market volatility and/or government financial reserves may not be adequate to address an adverse external event.

RISK RANKING

Nuclear Weapons State	Risk Score	Trend (+/- 0.5)	Risk Rank	Comments
Russia	1.5	+	2.0	
USA	4.0	O	4.0	Chinese economic aggression could trigger an economic crash in the U.S.
France	3.0	O	3.0	
China	2.0	O	2.0	
UK	3.5	-	3.0	
Israel	2.0	O	2.0	
Pakistan	3.0	O	3.0	
India	2.0	O	2.0	
N Korea	4.5	-	4.0	
Iran	2.0	O	2.0	

Survival Games

STRATEGIC UNDERMINING RISK FACTOR

DESCRIPTION	DISCUSSION
Strategic Undermining	This is a measure of the risk that a government's long term systemic financial condition may deteriorate sufficiently to force changes in vital interests and aggression or deterrence postures.

RANKING SCALE

LOW (1)	MEDIUM (3)	HIGH (5)
Government debt and entitlement liabilities are under control and funded by credible revenue projections.	Government debt and entitlement liabilities significantly exceed credible revenue projections but politically acceptable options are available to control the shortfalls.	Government debt and entitlement liabilities significantly exceed any conceivable revenue projections and no politically acceptable options are apparent that could prevent a coming crisis.

RISK RANKING

Nuclear Weapons State	Risk Score	Trend (+/- 0.5)	Risk Rank	Comments
Russia	2.0	O	2.0	
USA	5.0	O	5.0	See Appendix A
France	4.0	O	4.0	
China	2.5	O	2.0	
UK	4.5	-	4.0	Brexit uncertainty
Israel	2.0	O	2.0	
Pakistan	2.0	O	2.0	
India	2.0	O	2.0	
N Korea		O		Conditions are unknown
Iran	1.0	O	1.0	

92

Survival Games

ECONOMIC DISTRESS RISK FACTOR

DESCRIPTION	DISCUSSION
Economic Distress	This risk measures the likelihood that deteriorating economic conditions such as high unemployment, runaway inflation, or shortages of critical goods or services could force changes in vital interests and aggression or deterrence postures.

RANKING SCALE

LOW (1)	MEDIUM (3)	HIGH (5)
The economic stress is low with unemployment, inflation and GDP output within nominal levels.	The indicators of economic stress are clearly visible but are within experienced cyclical ranges and are responding to normal policy actions.	The indicators of economic stress are clearly visible, are outside of experienced cyclical ranges and/or are not responding to normal policy actions.

RISK RANKING

Nuclear Weapons State	Risk Score	Trend (+/- 0.5)	Risk Rank	Comments
Russia	2.0	O	2.0	
USA	1.5	+	2.0	
France	3.5	-	3.0	
China	3.0	O	3.0	
UK	2.0	O	2.0	
Israel	2.0	O	2.0	
Pakistan	3.0	O	3.0	
India	1.5	+	2.0	
N Korea	3.0	O	3.0	
Iran	2.0	+	2.0	

Exhibit 12-4 State Instability Risk Ranking Results

Nuclear Weapons State	Political Instability Risk	Economic Instability Risk	Combined Risk
Russia	2.60	1.90	2.60
United States	2.00	4.10	4.10
France	1.30	3.70	3.70
China	2.20	2.50	2.50
United Kingdom	1.60	3.80	3.80
Israel	1.20	2.00	2.00
Pakistan	3.40	2.40	3.40
India	2.20	1.90	2.20
North Korea	3.70	1.50	3.70
Iran	3.50	1.40	3.50

Risk ranking scale		
Low	Medium	High

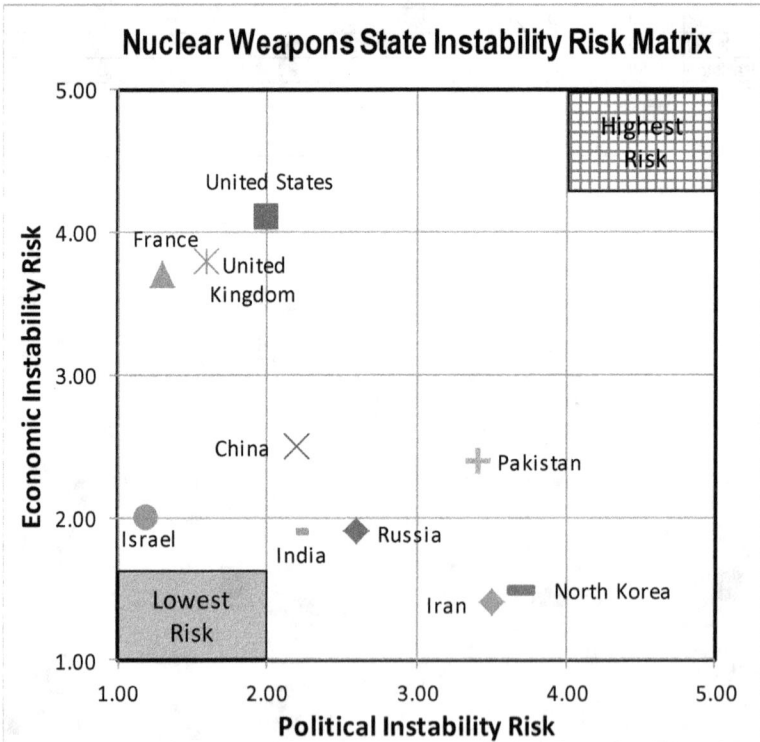

Nuclear Weapons State Instability Risk Matrix

The highest ranking given for political or economic risk was used as the combined instability risk. This method was used because either political or economic conditions could produce government instability. The results of this qualitative assessment indicate that the risk of political instability is medium for Russia, Pakistan and Iran and very high for North Korea. Economic instability risk was ranked high for France, the United Kingdom, and the United States.

The high instability ranking for N Korea flows from the inherent fragility of its hereditary dictatorship. These governments are typically very rigid and unchanging until they collapse entirely. The high instability rankings for France, the United Kingdom, and the United States came from high risk rankings for the "strategic undermining" metric. This was defined as a measure of the risk that a government's long term systemic financial condition may deteriorate sufficiently to force changes in vital interests and aggression or deterrence postures. The high risk ranking for this metric was assigned because I judged that these nations met the description for high strategic undermining risk which I defined as: *Government debt and entitlement liabilities significantly exceed any conceivable revenue projections and no politically acceptable options are apparent that could prevent a coming crisis.* This condition produces a form of unilateral disarmament that results when a government is unable to invest in the forces and equipment needed for its defense. To a significant degree, this has already happened in France and the United Kingdom with the deterrence shield for the democratic powers now funded almost entirely by the United States. As was already indicated, an uncontrolled weakening of the U.S. deterrence shield will invite adventurism from the autocratic nuclear weapons states and increase first strike risk across multiple conflict theaters.

The Unites States was also ranked high for economic fragility risk. This stems from the high level of sovereign debt and continuing deficits that have left the U.S. government vulnerable to insolvency if another economic crisis occurs. The Chinese government now has a large enough economy and sufficient financial reserves to deliberately wage economic war with the U.S. They could do this by suddenly putting all their accumulated U.S. treasury bonds up for sale. This would crash the global bond market, launch interest rates higher and make the further sale of bonds by the U.S. impossible. Faced with insolvency, the U.S. government would likely default on bond interest payments and redemptions. This would quickly lead to the failure of all international financial institutions which rely on these bonds as their primary "risk free" asset and the U.S. dollar as the reserve currency for financial transactions. Social unrest, political revolt, and calls for retribution against those responsible would follow at an unprecedented level of intensity. The possibility that these events could spin out of control and lead to war is significant.

The perilous financial condition of the U.S. government has been documented by many (see Appendix A References), but because of the importance of this finding to this risk assessment, I elected to go beyond the work of others and examine this issue independently. The results of this effort are presented in Appendix A. I defined a condition I call *debticide* and quantitatively defined it as the point in time when the U.S. government falls more than one trillion dollars behind the investment level needed to maintain the defense shield. I found that the U.S. will suffer debticide under a wide spectrum of economic conditions sometime between 2021 and 2034 with the most likely case being 2022. Please read Appendix A for a full description of this analysis.

The government instability risk ranking results were then used to modify the estimated first strike frequencies presented in Exhibit 11-8 in the previous chapter as follows. For nations that received a medium instability risk ranking, no change was made in the estimated first strike frequency. If the government instability risk ranking was low, then the first strike risk category was reduced one level in all affected conflict theaters. And, if the government instability risk ranking was high, then the first strike risk category was elevated one level in all affected conflict theaters. The following exhibit presents a summary of the adjustment process. The greatest impact of the state instability risk assessment was obviously the increase in estimated first strike frequencies for the United States.

Exhibit 12-5 Modified Nuclear First Strike Frequencies

Conflict Theater	Risk of First Strike from	First Strike Risk Ranking	Baseline Estimated Frequency	State Instability Ranking	Modified Frequency Estimate
Kashmir	India1	Med	3.0E-04	Low	3.1E-05
	Pakistan	Med	3.0E-04	Med	3.1E-04
Sikkim	India2	Med	3.0E-04	Low	3.1E-05
	China1	Med	3.0E-04	Med	3.1E-04
Korea	N Korea	Med	3.0E-04	High	3.1E-03
	USA1	Med	3.0E-04	High	3.1E-03
S China Sea	China2	Low	3.0E-05	Med	3.1E-05
	USA2	Low	3.0E-05	High	3.1E-04
Ukraine	Russia1	Low	3.0E-05	Med	3.1E-05
	NATO/USA3	Low	3.0E-05	High	3.1E-04
Baltics/ E Europe	Russia2	Low	3.0E-05	Med	3.1E-05
	NATO/USA4	Low	3.0E-05	High	3.1E-04
Syria/Iraq	Russia3	Med	3.0E-04	Med	3.1E-04
	NATO/USA5	Med	3.0E-04	High	3.1E-03
Israel	Iran	Low	3.0E-05	Med	3.1E-05
	Israel	Med	3.0E-04	Low	3.1E-05
Crashwar	China3	Med	3.0E-04	Med	3.1E-04
	USA6	Med	3.0E-04	High	3.1E-03

Proliferation Breakout

The instability I have discussed so far has focused on the current and anticipated nuclear weapons states. But another source of instability that could disturb the geopolitical equilibrium is the proliferation of nuclear weapons to nations outside of the group we have examined thus far. The danger inherent in nuclear weapons proliferation is obvious. Considerable international effort has been invested in this cause with the centerpiece being the Treaty on the Non-Proliferation of Nuclear Weapons (NPT). All nations except Israel, India, Pakistan, and N Korea are treaty signees. N Korea had signed the NPT in 1985 but withdrew in 2003. As a matter of formality, any future proliferators will at some point have to follow N Korea and withdraw as well. As of this time, Iran is the only expected cheater. One force that could cause a new round of proliferation is American debticide. If allies that have relied on the U.S. deterrent shield should begin to feel vulnerable, they may consider the need to defend themselves. I doubt that anyone reading this book would be surprised to learn that a fair number of industrialized democracies have the technical capability to become nuclear weapons states very quickly, if the need should arise. In addition, the non-NPT members are capable of covertly marketing nuclear technology. If the current proliferation equilibrium should be broken by even one state, it would be likely to start a proliferation breakout of many new players. I have no way to predict such an event or describe what the consequences might be. So for now, this possibility is acknowledged but will remain outside the scope of the MFRA2.

Part V - Mega Fatality Risk Assessment Update

My objective in this part of the book is to present all the material you will need to understand the updated Mega Fatality Risk Assessment (MFRA2) as a stand-alone assessment. I am not repeating all the background on risk assessment methods and tools that is presented in *Risk Management Revisited*, but I have included the glossary of risk management terms from *RMR* as Appendix C to help if a quick reminder is needed. Still you may need to consult *RMR* if you need more depth on risk assessment methodology.

Chapter 13 - Research on Other Risk Contributors

In addition to the research on human conflict presented in Parts II, III, and IV, a review and updated data search was conducted for all important contributors to the original MFRA results. This chapter discusses the significant findings of this effort.

Pandemic Risk

All deaths attributed to pandemics were included in the MFRA results. No attempt was made to identify pandemics whose consequences fell below the threshold of one million fatalities within 90 days that defines a mega fatality event. This approach was not important for a demonstration assessment, but it presents a problem for the comparison of background individual risk and mega fatality risk presented in Chapter 16. Crosschecking our official list of pandemics against the 2015 mortality data reveals that most, if not all deaths from recent pandemics are recorded in the annual mortality data. In our data sample year of 2015, only four communicable diseases killed one million or more globally for the whole year with the largest being pneumonia. So the preponderance of pandemics counted in the MFRA do not qualify as true mega fatality events. In recent history, only the flu pandemics of 1918, 1957, and 1968, plus HIV/AIDS register as high intensity, uncontrolled, mega fatality events. Also, the most severe, the 1918 flu, occurred before antibiotics and vaccines, so this large a death toll may not be a good predictor of future outcomes.

So I thought it would be appropriate to review the totality of pandemic risk that is included in the updated assessment. The MFRA2 includes five possible causes of high intensity pandemics. The *natepid* initiating event is retained from the MFRA to allow for the occurrence of a naturally occurring high intensity pathogen. The frequency has been reduced to account for the fact that most communicable disease deaths are not mega fatality events and are recorded in the annual mortality data. Containment failure probability was reduced to acknowledge that health care systems have established a record of high effectiveness. Conditional consequence estimates are unchanged from the original MFRA.

The accidental release of a known pathogen from a BSL-4 lab (*bioaccident*) is included at the same frequency used in the MFRA. My assessment that this scenario is a significant risk contributor based on the disturbing number of precursor accidents that have occurred remains unchanged. The updated assessment of pandemics caused by terrorism, *biolabsab* and *bioattack* is discussed in the "Treatment of Terrorism" section that comes later.

The fifth and possibly most important cause of pandemic deaths comes from events where medical services organizations are unable to act or are deliberately prevented from acting to contain and treat the spread of infectious diseases. Medical service personnel are after all just people and when they are impacted by war, electric power outages, severe environmental conditions, or other events, they cannot perform their work at a normal level. This is part of the societal life support systems breakdown (*chaos*) that results from many of the MFRA scenarios. In these conditions, starvation, disease, exposure, and unchecked violence may all be acting in concert to produce calamitous results.

Long Term Electric Power Outages

The importance of long term electric power outages was a major finding of the MFRA. Three very different causes for long term electric power outages were identified in the MFRA; solar storms, direct sabotage, and nuclear electromagnetic pulse (EMP) weapons. Additional research produced new information relevant to both the frequency and consequences of these events.

New research (Reference 22) provided the basis for lowering the frequency of severe solar storms but increasing the potential size and severity of the resulting electric power outage. Analysis and evidence suggests that a coronal mass ejection (CME) significantly stronger that the 1859 Carrington event is possible and could produce global effects with nations nearest both poles affected most severely. An updated and lower frequency for direct sabotage of electric power systems is discussed in the section on the treatment of terrorism. The likelihood of EMP weapons use was quantified in the MFRA without identification of specific attackers or targets. The increased fidelity for nuclear war modeling in the MFRA2 now allows this to be done. The results produced from this more detailed analysis of nuclear war are reported in Chapter 16.

A research need identified in the MFRA was for the development of a systematic method for estimating the human fatality consequences that would result from a widespread and extended electric power outage in a high tech society. This research is still needed, but I was able to find some additional evidence relevant to this question.

First, because of geography, the threat of an EMP attack seems especially real for the U.S. and North America. To produce the desired effects, an EMP weapon must be detonated at a high altitude, producing widespread damage over an area more than a thousand miles in diameter. This fact largely prevents the U.S. from retaliating in kind for an EMP attack because of the collateral damage that would be felt by U.S. allies in Asia or Europe but leaves the autocratic nuclear weapons nations with a clear fire zone over North America. This geographical advantage might lead one of the autocratic nuclear weapons states to rationalize that an EMP attack combined with the threat of a strategic attack might cause the U.S. to capitulate rather than retaliate with strategic weapons for the EMP attack.

Next, a study done by the U.S. Department of Energy on the reliability of large power transformers (Reference 20) reveals that

- There are estimated to be well over 10,000 large power transformers in the U.S. with new additions averaging about 250 each year.
- Large power transformer manufacturing is now centered in Asia and Europe.
- U.S. domestic transformer manufacturing capacity can only supply about 15% of domestic demand for large transformers or less than 50 units per year

Thus, if any significant fraction of the U.S. large power transformer fleet is destroyed by any of our initiators, full recovery may take a very long time.

Finally, although the public reports from the U.S. commission to assess the EMP threat (References 30 & 31) do not provide any quantitative estimate of potential fatalities that could be caused by an EMP attack, comments made by the commissioners following completion of the reports indicate that there are classified versions of the reports and that they may contain fatality estimates that project the loss of life in the U.S. in the year following an EMP attack to reach 60% or more of the population. This is much higher than was estimated in the MFRA.

Unfortunately, these new data points indicate that the consequences of a long term electric power outage may be worse than estimated in the MFRA.

The Treatment of Terrorism

Various approaches were used in the MFRA to estimate the likelihood of terrorist attacks and the model architecture allowed for the possibility of these attacks escalating to war. In the MFRA2, the likelihood that terrorist actions lead to war is encompassed by the initiating event frequencies estimated for conventional and nuclear war. However, there is still the possibility that a terrorist attack itself could result in a mega fatality event, even if no greater war follows. To account for such events, four initiators were retained in the MFRA2. They are:

- *epsabotage* – This is the direct sabotage of an electric power system producing an outage of extended duration.
- *biolabsab* – This is the sabotage and deliberate release of high severity pathogens from a BSL-4 research laboratory.
- *bioattack* – This is the deliberate release of a weaponized pathogen produced independently by a terrorist organization.
- *nucdet* – This is the detonation of a nuclear weapon constructed by a terrorist organization in a high population area.

In reviewing the risk contributions of these events to our analysis, I felt the need to improve the rationale for and consistency among the initiating event frequencies used for these events. I know that attributing rationality to terrorists is a tenuous proposition, but here it goes. The following table presents the relative merits of these attack methods, from a terrorist's point of view.

Exhibit 13-1 Terrorist Attack Initiators

Terrorist Event	Planning & Execution	Consequences
epsabotage (1.25E-2)	No sophisiticated weapons or equipment needed. Probably requires the largest attack team but the least sophisticated.	Damage is done only to selected target and may be extensive. Has the least dramatic terror effects.
biolabsab (5.62E-3)	A well trained attack team and good intelligence about the target are needed. No special weapons or equipment needed.	The scope of damage that results is uncertain. Severity should be greatest in the target country, but disease could spread widely, even to the terrorist homeland.
bioattack (6.25E-4)	Requires significant scientific and technical personnel and laboratory facilities plus difficult to obtain input materials.	The scope of damage that results is uncertain. Severity should be greatest in the target country, but disease could spread widely, even to the terrorist homeland.
nucdet (6.25E-3)	Requires significant scientific and technical personnel and laboratory facilities plus by far the most difficult to obtain input materials.	Damage is done only to selected target and will be extensive. Has by far the most dramatic terror effects.

All the terrorist acts listed above require long term, large team planning and execution and a good degree of technical competence. Terrorists have definitely exhibited a preference in recent years for small team, low tech attacks. So what frequency should we assign to the likelihood of events like those discussed above? No large team terrorist attack has been launched against a high tech nation since 9/11/2001. Sixteen years with no such attacks indicates that the expected frequency for any attack is in the range of 2.5E-2 per year. We will assign half of this frequency to the easiest of the terrorist attacks to execute, epsabotage. Next we will assign one quarter of this frequency to nucdet because it has the highest terror value but is the most difficult. The remaining one quarter we will split 90/10 between biolabsab and bioattack. These target frequencies are listed in the exhibit above and will be used in the MFRA2 update, with considerable uncertainty.

Global Cooling Consequences

Research into the effects of nuclear weapons use detailed in Part III indicate that very severe global fatality levels may result from global cooling caused by debris driven high into the atmosphere by the detonation of a large number of nuclear weapons. Since asteroid/comet strikes and large explosive volcanic eruptions also result in similar debris elevation and global cooling, the event tree end states defined for all these events were integrated as is described in Chapter 14.

Chapter 14 - The MFRA2 Event Tree Model

The architecture of the MFRA2 risk model depicted in Exhibit 1-2 is that of an *event tree* model. Event tree modeling is the most direct and understandable method for quantitative risk analysis. An event tree is simply a diagram that logically resolves all possible outcomes from a causally ordered series of events. Event trees start from an *initiating event* and are typically drawn from left to right with the causal events (called *top events*) listed as questions at top of the diagram. At each top event, the event tree path divides into two or more branches depending on the outcome of the top event with the straight or up branch generally representing success and the down branch generally representing failure. Each unique path through the event tree defines a *scenario* and the condition resulting from the successes and failures of the top events in the scenario is called an *end state*. End states are potentially unique but in practice a limited number of end state categories are defined and used for collecting results.

The event tree quantification process begins with an initiating event frequency (events/unit of time). The values assigned at each branch point to the down branch are called *split fractions* (SF) and the values used for the straight branch are complements (1-SF). The split fractions are conditional probabilities and are dependent on the occurrence of the initiator and all the top events that precede the split fraction in the event tree structure. Since the split fractions at each top event always add to 1.0, the scenario results will be frequencies that sum to the value of the initiator. The exhibit below shows one of our more simple event trees complete with mean value quantitative results. The numbers in this example are shown using scientific notation which is very handy for expressing very large or very small numbers. For example, 6.9E-03 is shorthand for 0.0069. Also, the abbreviations "GYes" or "GNo" indicate that the answer to a top event question is guaranteed to be yes or no.

Exhibit 14-1 Example Event Tree

Initiator	Containment Effective?	SLS systems maintained?	#	Frequency (events/yr)	End State	Risk (PF/yr)
bioaccident	Yes	GYes	1	4.71E-02	pand4	4.56E+05
	CFH	Yes	2	9.39E-04	pand5	6.06E+04
		SLSP	3	9.39E-04	pand5+	1.09E+05
				4.90E-02		6.25E+05

The "GYes" and "GNo" abbreviations shown at some branch points indicate that the answer to the top event question is guaranteed to be yes or no. The software that I used to construct and calculate risk model results is *Microsoft Excel* with an add-in Monte Carlo simulation tool from Oracle Corporation called *Crystal Ball*. *Crystal Ball* allows the values in the spreadsheet cells to be probability distributions instead of point values. It will also combine distributions using the Monte Carlo method and place the resulting distribution in a designated cell. Cells containing distributions are highlighted in the spreadsheet pages shown in Appendix B. I have not included listings of the actual equations used or probability distribution details since these require familiarity with the software to understand.

MFRA2 Model Architecture and Organization

The basic architecture of the MFRA2 scenario model remains the same as depicted in Exhibit 1-2. The primary change in model structure for the MFRA2 is in the approach to modelling nuclear war. In the MFRA, nuclear war was modeled to result from the escalation of a non-nuclear conflict. In the MFRA2, 17 specific initiating events were identified for nuclear war as described in Part IV. This produced a MFRA2 scenario model with simpler architecture but significantly more initiating events and total scenarios.

After incorporating these changes in war modeling and the research on other events previously discussed, the initiating events evaluated in the MFRA2 are as follows.

Exhibit 14-2 MFRA2 Initiating Events

Initiator		Calculated Mean	Source References
Code	Description		
Cosmic Events			
KI10m	Kinetic impact of 10 m object	1.3E-01	Reference #2
KI100m	Kinetic impact of 100 m object	3.2E-04	Reference #2
KI1km	Kinetic impact of 1 km object	5.7E-06	Reference #2
KI10km	Kinetic impact of 10 km object	4.0E-08	Reference #2
SolStrm	Solar storm	3.7E-03	Reference #22
Natural Terrestrial Events			
SuperV7	VEI category 7 volcanic eruption	2.7E-05	Reference #10
SuperV8	VEI category 8 volcanic eruption	8.2E-06	Reference #10
Mquake	Mega Earthquake	9.3E-01	Reference #13
Mflood	Other flood event	3.5E-03	Reference #14
Pandemic Events			
NatEpid	High severity natural epidemic	4.4E-02	Chapter 14
bioaccident	Accidental release of known disease	4.9E-02	Chapter 14
bioattack	Release of weaponized pathogen	6.8E-04	Chapter 13
biolabsab	Biological laboratory sabotage	6.1E-03	Chapter 13
Terrorist Attacks			
epsabotage	Electric power system sabotage	1.4E-02	Chapter 13
nucdet	Nuclear terrorist attack	6.8E-03	Chapter 13
Human Conflict			
armcon	Conventional armed conflict	3.08	Chapter 2
lofw	Nuclear first strike on false warning	5.8E-04	Chapter 9
India1	Nuclear first strike by India1	3.0E-05	Chapter 11 & 12
Pakistan	Nuclear first strike by Pakistan	3.0E-04	Chapter 11 & 12
India2	Nuclear first strike by India2	3.0E-05	Chapter 11 & 12
China1	Nuclear first strike by China1	3.0E-05	Chapter 11 & 12
N Korea	Nuclear first strike by N Korea	3.0E-03	Chapter 11 & 12
USA1	Nuclear first strike by USA1	3.0E-03	Chapter 11 & 12
China2	Nuclear first strike by China2	3.0E-05	Chapter 11 & 12
USA2	Nuclear first strike by USA2	3.0E-04	Chapter 11 & 12
Russia1	Nuclear first strike by Russia1	3.0E-05	Chapter 11 & 12
NATO/USA3	Nuclear first strike by USA3	3.0E-04	Chapter 11 & 12
Russia2	Nuclear first strike by Russia2	3.0E-05	Chapter 11 & 12
NATO/USA4	Nuclear first strike by USA4	3.0E-04	Chapter 11 & 12
Russia3	Nuclear first strike by Russia3	3.0E-04	Chapter 11 & 12
NATO/USA5	Nuclear first strike by USA5	3.0E-03	Chapter 11 & 12
Iran	Nuclear first strike by Iran	3.0E-05	Chapter 11 & 12
Israel	Nuclear first strike by Israel	3.0E-05	Chapter 11 & 12
China3	Nuclear first strike by China3	3.0E-04	Chapter 11 & 12
USA6	Nuclear first strike by USA6	3.0E-03	Chapter 11 & 12

And the top event split fraction codes used in the event tree structures are as follows.

Exhibit 14-3 MFRA2 Top Event Split Fractions

	Initiator	calculated	
Code	Description	Mean	Source References
HPZ	Probability of impact in high population zone	0.03	550 cities w > 1M people, a hit within a 50 mi radius of each gives a target of 4.3 mil sq mi or ~ 2%
LAND	Probability of impact on land	0.29	
SF	Bio lab security measures fail to prevent release	0.50	JPK estimate
CFH	Containment failure for high severity pathogen	0.04	JPK estimate
CFX	Containment failure following bio lab attack	0.19	JPK estimate
CFXX	Containment failure following bio attack	0.38	
SLSP	Failure of SLS systems during pandemic	0.50	JPK estimate
SLSEP	Failure of SLS systems during extended EP outage	0.50	JPK estimate
EPCW	EP sabotage results in continent wide outage	0.38	JPK estimate
NWHY	Terrorist nuclear weapon is high yield	0.05	JPK estimate
CW	Probability that a mega conflict is a civil war	0.70	14/20
MEGAC	Probability of mega fatality conflict	3.18E-02	20/630
DCW	Probability of democide in a civil war	0.42	6/14
GC1	Probability of global cooling with <100 weapons	0.00	
GC2	Probability of global cooling with <250 weapons	0.57	

In the balance of this Chapter, I will discuss the construction of the event trees, the development of split fraction conditional probabilities and the assignment of scenario end states. All these elements of the MFRA risk model with numeric values can also be found in the risk model worksheets provided in Appendix B. For the most part, I will not repeat the numeric values from the risk model in the text, so you might want make copies of some of the key data tables to facilitate following along as you read. In Chapter 15, I will describe the definition of scenario end state codes that are listed in the event trees and the development of probability distributions for prompt fatality consequences. Finally, in Chapter 16, I will summarize and review the results of the MFRA2.

Cosmic Events

Random asteroid/comet strike on Earth (KI10m, KI100M, KI1km,KI10km)

We begin our discussion of the MFRA model with kinetic impact events. I found that both the frequency and direct impacts of potential kinetic impact events to have been comprehensively researched (References 1-4). I elected to model kinetic impacts by defining four categories of events based on object size with frequencies as listed in Exhibit 14-2.

First, for smaller size objects with a nominal diameter of 10 meters (KI10m), significant fatalities should only be produced if the object impacts near a high population area. To estimate this likelihood, I added a top event question in the KI10m event tree to ask for the conditional probability of a kinetic impact near a high population zone. The split fraction for the conditional probability of a high population zone impact (HPZ) was estimated by assuming that a 10 meter object must strike within 50 miles of a high population area to produce significant prompt fatalities (PF). With an estimated 550 target cities with populations greater than one million on the Earth, I calculated the conditional probability of a high population zone hit (HPZ) at about 2%.

For a strike by larger size objects with nominal diameters of 100 meters (KI100m), 1 kilometer (KI1km), or 10 kilometers (KI10km) direct blast and impact effects will be observed on a local (KI100m) or regional (KI1km) scale. In addition, debris ejected into the upper atmosphere from the larger size impacts is expected to produce significant global cooling depending on the size of the impactor and impact location with land strikes producing much greater climate effects than water impacts. Because of this, the event trees for the larger asteroid strikes question the impact location and adjust the end state consequences accordingly. The structure of the kinetic impact event trees is presented in the next exhibit.

Exhibit 14-4 Kinetic Impact Event Trees

Initiator	Impact in low population area?	#	End State
KI10m	Yes	1	nomega
	HPZ	2	PF10m

Initiator	Water Impact?	#	End State
KI100m	Yes	1	PF100m
	LAND	2	gcm

Initiator	Water Impact?	#	End State
KI1km	Yes	1	gcm
	LAND	2	gcs

Initiator	Water Impact?	#	End State
KI10km	Yes	1	gcs
	LAND	2	gcc

The KI10km event was also used in the MFRA as a cutoff frequency to eliminate less likely events. Since the KI10km event yields human extinction at a mean frequency of about 1E-8, it effectively provides a frequency floor for the risk analysis. Events with frequencies less than 1E-8, no matter how severe, cannot significantly contribute to the risk results because of the floor created by KI10km. As a result, events such as attacks by aliens or artificial life forms do not appear in our risk analysis.

Solar electromagnetic storm (SolStrm)

In addition to the normal energy output that makes the Earth habitable, the sun routinely fires out extra bursts of energy that can be harmful if they strike Earth. These bursts of energy or solar storms consist of three major components: solar flares, solar proton events (SPEs) and coronal mass ejections (CMEs). Not all solar storms produce all three elements but the largest solar storms do. The most severe solar storm recorded in recent history occurred on August 28 through September 2, 1859. This is called the Carrington Event named after British astronomer Richard Carrington who actually witnessed the instigating solar flare. Electromagnetic energy from this solar storm electrified telegraph lines, shocking technicians and setting their telegraph papers on fire. Other observed impacts included the Northern Lights spreading as far south as Cuba and Hawaii and auroras over the Rocky Mountains so bright that they woke campers because they thought it was morning.

As was discussed in Chapter 13, solar storms are the first of three initiators included in the MFRA2 that can cause extended electric power system outages. Reference 21 gives a good overview of solar storm physics and the damage they can do to electrical systems. I have used the latest and I think best estimate for the frequency of solar storms equal to or greater than the Carrington event given by Reference 22. In addition, much of the analysis and testing done to assess the risk of an EMP attack is also applicable to solar storms.

Because of our increased reliance on electric and electronic systems, a similar solar storm today would have a much more severe impact on society that it did in 1859. A loss of electric power and societal life support systems dependent on electric power for months or years would be experienced over at least the region of Earth most directly impacted by the solar storm. The size of the area impacted could vary significantly depending on the strength of the storm and the directness of the strike on the Earth. As a result, the event tree for solar storms merely divides out the area impacted into categories that match the "chaos" end states defined later. The highest probability is given to the second scenario as shown in the event tree below.

Exhibit 14-5 Solar Storm Event Tree

Initiator	EP outage extent?	#	End State	Comments
SolStrm	0.25	1	chaos2	national EP outage
	0.45	2	chaos3	continental EP outage
	0.25	3	chaos4	hemispheric EP outage
	0.05	4	chaos5	global EP outage

Natural Terrestrial Events

Super volcanic eruption (SuperV7 & SuperV8)

Volcanic eruptions occur often and can be quite spectacular, but they seldom cause significant human deaths because the ground motion, lava, and ash flows are generally local in nature and not near high population zones. It is possible, however, for an eruption to be so violent that the mass ejected reaches the upper atmosphere and disperses to blot out the sunlight. The resulting cooling could last for an extended period impacting multiple food crop cycles. If severe enough, regional and global failure of societal life support systems could occur and result in significant human fatalities.

To gauge this risk, a volcanic explosivity index (VEI) has been defined to measure the severity of eruptions. The VEI contains nine levels designated zero through 8. Ejecta from VE-1 through 6 eruptions is capable of producing short term effects such as air travel disruption but only VEI-7 & 8 are potentially severe enough to cause lasting regional or global cooling. The only eruption in this severity range to occur in modern times was the VEI-7 eruption of Mount Tambora in Indonesia in 1815. Global cooling was experienced through 1816 and is known as the year without summer. Frequencies for these events were estimated using data from Reference #5. Top events were also included in the event trees for SuperV7 and SuperV8 to assess the severity of global cooling that might result from these events.

Great earthquake and/or tsunami (Mquake)

Large earthquakes are actually quite common with quakes of magnitude 8 or 9 occurring at a rate of almost one per year, per

USGS data (Reference 8). Per the USGS data, no earthquake/tsunami has yet killed enough people to meet the one million prompt fatalities threshold for the MFRA. But with human populations steadily increasing, especially in areas where little investment is made in seismic risk reduction, I think it is only a matter of time until this unfortunate threshold is met.

For the MFRA2, the USGS historical data indicating that 89 M8 and M9 earthquakes have occurred in the last 113 years was used to establish the initiating event frequency, and then I included a top event to ask if the quake occurred near a high population area, similar to KI10m. The end state "equake" was assigned to the scenario where a severe earthquake impacts a high population area and the resulting distribution for prompt fatalities is described in Chapter 15.

Exceptionally severe cyclone/hurricane or other flood (Mflood)
I chose to aggregate all types of flooding events, other than tsunamis, together under this initiator for the MFRA risk model. Reference 9 indicates that the only historical flood events to meet our fatalities criteria have been river floods. It may be that the seemingly more severe cyclones/hurricanes present less risk because people typically have advanced warning of their arrival allowing time for evacuation while river floods caused by a dam or levy break can strike with little warning. In any case, the initiating event frequency is based on data for three events in approximately the last 1000 years that did meet our one million fatalities criteria. Therefore the impact on a high population zone is guaranteed at this frequency.

Extreme drought or other food crop failure and famine
Despite many warnings, food production in modern times has been fully able to keep pace with an increasing human population. A review of the historical data for famine events indicates that the most severe famines have been consequences of other events such as war and democide. These other events

brought about what I characterize in the MFRA2 risk model as a breakdown of societal life support systems. The "chaos" end states defined in Chapter 15 represent this condition. Under chaos conditions, starvation, disease, exposure, and unchecked violence may all be acting in concert to produce calamitous results. As a result, I chose to account for famine in the MFRA2 risk model as a consequence of other events rather than an independent initiating event.

Exhibit 14-6 Natural Terrestrial Event Trees

Super Volcano events

Initiator	Global cooling?	#	End State
SuperV7	No	1	chaos1
	moderate (.5)	2	gcm

Initiator	Global cooling?	#	End State
SuperV8	moderate	1	gcm
	severe (.5)	2	gcs

Mega Earthquake

Initiator	Impact in low population area?	#	End State
Mquake	Yes	1	nomega
	HPZ	2	equake

Mega Flood

Initiator	Impact in low population area?	#	End State
Mflood	GNo	1	flood

Pandemic Events

Naturally Occurring Pandemic (natepid)

The change in modeling approach used for naturally occurring pandemics in the MFRA2 was described in Chapter 13. A review of the list of pandemics used to develop the MFRA initiating event frequency against the 2015 mortality data revealed that most, if not all deaths from recent pandemics, are not mega fatality events and are recorded in the annual mortality data. In our data sample year of 2015, only four communicable diseases killed one million or more globally for the whole year with the largest being pneumonia. So the preponderance of pandemics counted in the MFRA do not qualify as mega fatality events. In recent history, only the flu pandemics of 1918, 1957, and 1968, plus HIV/AIDS register as high intensity, mega fatality events. Also, the most severe, the 1918 flu, occurred before antibiotics and vaccines, so this large a death toll may not be a good predictor of future outcomes. Still, these four pandemics having occurred over the last century are definitive data points and now establish the median of the *natepid* at 0.04 per year.

As a result of the changes discussed above, all *natepid* scenarios are now mega fatality events. The event tree still questions the likelihood that medical services are able to successfully prevent a runaway outbreak (top event CFH) and, if not, then asks if societal life support systems are maintained (top event SLSP). The values for these split fractions were judged to be low, meaning that for the most likely scenario (natepid1) the disease spread would remain under sufficient control to prevent any panic. The development of end state probability distributions for prompt fatalities is described in Chapter 15.

Accidental release of known disease (bioaccident)

I developed the frequency for this initiator by assuming that an accidental biological release capable of causing a high intensity pandemic was most likely to originate from a biosafety level 4 (BSL-4) laboratory. Per reference #51 there are currently 42 such facilities worldwide. References #57 through #65 chronical additional precursor events which have already occurred that narrowly missed producing serious consequences. And I am not using the term serious lightly. Per reference #58, "between 1978 and 1999, just over 1,200 people acquired infections from BSL-4 labs around the world; 22 were fatal. Since then, lab workers have been killed by Ebola and SARS, or severe acquired respiratory syndrome. Thieves tried to steal animal pathogens from an Indonesian lab in 2007." Based on this information I assigned a mean release frequency of 0.001 per year (once in a thousand years) for each facility. This yields a total release frequency of 0.042 per year. I then represented the uncertainty with a triangular distribution that ranged from 0.021 to 0.84 per year.

The event tree structure for *bioaccident* is the same as *natepid*. Since the identity of the released pathogen should be immediately known, the likelihood of containment should be good, even though it may be difficult to control. As a result, the same split fractions and end state assignments used for natural pandemics are used here. The development of end state probability distributions for prompt fatalities is described in Chapter 15.

Biological laboratory sabotage (biolabsab)
Biological weapon attack (bioattack)
The initiating event frequencies for biological laboratory sabotage and biological attack were derived from the total assessment of terrorist attack risk presented in Chapter 13. A higher likelihood for bio lab sabotage was allocated relative to bio attack because of evidence indicating that security at these facilities is poor. Thus, if potential bio terrorists were rational, they would take deadly pathogens from a BSL-4 facility and release them rather than bother producing their own. Especially concerning was a research piece done by Reuters (Reference #52). This article describes safety and especially security requirements that I found alarming. Having spent nearly 40 years working in nuclear technology including serving as a Group Leader at Los Alamos National Laboratory, I have some familiarity with nuclear security requirements. After reading that the BSL-4 labs contain stores of deadly pathogens designated as

"select agents" because they are fatal to humans and have no known vaccine or treatment, I expected to find nuclear class (or better) safety and security requirements in place. Not even close. In the United States, BSL-4 labs are located within high population areas (Atlanta) and, in at least one case, in an area with significant natural phenomena hazards (Galveston, Texas - hurricanes). Nuclear facilities would not be allowed in these locations. In addition, the operational security provisions described in reference #52 would only compare with those for the unclassified areas of Los Alamos.

The event tree structures for *biolabsab* and *bioattack* are much the same as *natepid*. One additional top event was added to *biolabsab* to allow for the possibility that lab security measures are successful in preventing a pathogen release during an attack. Since the identity of the released pathogen(s) may not be immediately known, split fractions with higher likelihoods of medical containment failure (CFX and CFXX) were used for these initiators. The development of end state probability distributions for prompt fatalities is described in Chapter 15.

Exhibit 14-7 Biological Event Trees

Initiator	Med Containment Effective?	SLS Systems Maintained?	#	End State
Natepid	Yes	GYes	1	pand4
0.04	CFH	Yes	2	pand5
		SLSP	3	pand5+

Initiator	Med Containment Effective?	SLS systems maintained?	#	End State
bioaccident	Yes	GYes	1	pand4
	CFH	Yes	2	pand5
		SLSP	3	pand5+

Initiator	Security measures effective?	Med Containment Effective?	SLS systems maintained?	#	End State
biolabsab	Yes	n/a	n/a	1	nomega
	SF	Yes	GYes	2	pand4
		CFX	Yes	3	pand5
			SLSP	4	pand5+

Initiator	Med Containment Effective?	SLS systems maintained?	#	End State
bioattack	Yes	GYes	1	pand4
	CFXX	Yes	2	pand5
		SLSP	3	pand5+

Acts of Terrorism

Electric power system sabotage (epsabotage)
Nuclear terrorist attack (nucdet)

The approach used to model terrorism risk in the MFRA2 and the development of initiating event frequencies for attack events was presented in Chapter 13. Event trees for the two terrorist attacks that could produce pandemics were presented in the previous section because of their commonalities with other pandemic events.

The event tree for electric power system sabotage *(epsabotage)* is shown below. Top event questions are included to determine the scope or extent of the outage and whether or not other societal life support systems can be maintained in the absence of electric power. Values for the split fractions EPCW and SLSEP used here are based on my judgement. A much more significant chance of SLS success was allowd here compared to solar storm and EMP events though because electronic systems and communications systems will lose power but not be directly damaged by a sabotage attack. This may allow a faster and easier recovery than would be possible for the other events. All scenarios are assigned to one of the "chaos" family of end states as defined in Chapter 15.

Exhibit 14-8 EP Sabotage Event Tree

Initiator	Scope of outage limited?	SLS systems maintained?	#	End State
epsabotage	Yes	Yes	1	chaos1
		SLSEP	2	chaos2
	EPCW	Yes	3	chaos2
		SLSEP	4	chaos3

The event tree for a nuclear terrorist attack *(nucdet)* merely asks one question to determine the yield range of the weapon for assigning end state categories. End states for nuclear detonations were developed using the guidelines developed in Chapter 6.

Exhibit 14-9 Terrorist Nuclear Attack Event Tree

Initiator	Low yield weapon?	#	End State
nucdet	Yes	1	nucattack
	NWHY	2	nucattackp

Human Conflict

As discussed earlier and listed in Exhibit 14-2, war in the MFRA2 is modeled with 16 initiating events, one for conventional armed conflict and 15 for nuclear war. All non-nuclear warfare is modeled in the armed conflict *(armcon)* event tree. The frequency of conventional armed conflicts between 1950 and 2010 presented in Chapter 2 is used as the median frequency for this initiator. The *armcon* event tree contains the following three top event questions.

1. Mega fatality conflict?
This top event questions asks if the conflict reaches the one million casualty level need to qualify as a mega fatality event. Per the data in Chapter 2, only 20 out of 630 (3.18%) conflicts documented since 1800 passed this threshold. As a result, the lion's share of armed conflict frequency is routed down on this event tree branch to scenario armcon4, which is not a mega fatality end state.

2. Multi-national war?
This top event questions asks if the conflict is a multi-national or civil war. Per the data presented in Chapter 2, 14 out of 20 (70%) of the documented mega fatality conflicts can best be characterized as civil wars.

3. Democide?
Since democide is defined as a government exterminating its own people, it is modeled as a form of civil war. Six of the 14 mega fatality civil wars documented in Chapter 2 could also be classified as democides.

The end states for scenarios armcon1, 2, and 3 are unique to mega fatality interstate war (iswardths), mega fatality civil war plus democide (demodths), and mega fatality civil war (cwdths), respectively. The distributions for these end states are developed in Chapter 15.

Exhibit 14-10 Armed Conflict Event Tree

Initiator	Mega Fatality Conflict?	Multi-National War?	Democide?	#	End State
armcon	MEGAC	Yes	n/a	1	iswardths
		CW	DCW	2	demodths
			No	3	cwdths
	No	n/a	GNo	4	nomega

Nuclear First Strike on False Warning

The likelihood of a nuclear first strike by Russia or the USA in response to a false warning of attack was described in Chapter 9. The event tree top event questions for this initiator merely asks what the number of warheads launched actually becomes before the mistake is realized and the conflict ended. Although these are legitimate questions for the event, we have no basis to answer them with any odds other than 50/50. For the worst case scenario lofw3, Reference #70 indicates that a total of over 1700 warheads are on launch ready status between Russia and the USA and could be used. This is the first event tree to use the warhead (**whd**) series of end states. The development of prompt fatality distributions for these end states is described in Chapter 15.

Exhibit 14-11 Launch on False Warning Event Tree

Initiator	<10 warheads launched?	<100 warheads launched?	#	End State
lofw	Yes	n/a	1	swhd10
	0.5	Yes	2	swhd100
		0.5	3	gcs

Nuclear First Strike

Nuclear first strike with intent is modeled with 16 potential initiating events as described in Chapters 11 and 12. The nuclear first strike event trees all use the same three top event questions:

1. First strike weapons used?

If the nuclear first strike event trees were fully developed to answer this questions and the next, the scenario combinations would become quite complex and contain a difficult to manage number of scenarios. To simplify the size and complexity of the event tree models without sacrificing important outcomes, the type of nuclear weapons used for a first strike was assigned using the following rules:

- India, Pakistan, Israel, and Iran are assumed to have only strategic weapons, so the likelihood of tactical or EMP weapons use is zero.
- The first strike weapons of preference for the USA are tactical since this allows for the possibility of a limited nuclear war with relatively low casualties and the capitulation of the adversary without retaliation.
- The first strike weapons of preference to be used by all adversaries against the USA are EMP since they can be used over North America without concern for collateral damage to allies. This also allows for the possibility of a limited nuclear war with relatively low direct casualties and the capitulation of the adversary without retaliation.

2. Retaliation weapons used?

This question features multiple branch points and allows for the attacked state to respond with any available type of nuclear weapon, or none. The split fraction values are based on my judgement as listed in the next exhibit.

Exhibit 14-12 Nuclear Retaliation Likelihood Values

First Strike by:	First strike weapons used?	Retaliation weapons used?	Split fraction value	Comments
N Korea	EMP	tactical	0.8	Tactical weapons should be adequate to defeat NK
		strategic	0.1	
		none	0.1	
USA1	tactical	tactical	0	
		EMP	0.2	
		strategic	0.2	
		none	0.6	NK unlikely to be able to retaliate
China	EMP	tactical	0.8	
		strategic	0.1	
		none	0.1	China may capitulate
USA2		tactical	0.2	
		EMP	0.4	
		strategic	0.2	
		none	0.2	US may capitulate
Russia1	EMP	tactical	0.4	
		strategic	0.1	
		none	0.5	US may capitulate
NATO/USA3	tactical	tactical	0.2	
		EMP	0.4	
		strategic	0.4	
		none	0	
Russia2	EMP	tactical	0.8	
		strategic	0.1	
		none	0.1	US may capitulate
NATO/USA4	tactical	tactical	0.2	
		EMP	0.4	
		strategic	0.4	
		none	0	
Russia3	EMP	tactical	0.8	
		strategic	0.1	
		none	0.1	US may capitulate
NATO/USA5	tactical	tactical	0.2	
		EMP	0.4	
		strategic	0.4	
		none	0	
China3	EMP	tactical	0.8	
		strategic	0.1	
		none	0.1	China may capitulate
USA6		tactical	0.2	
		EMP	0.4	
		strategic	0.2	
		none	0.2	US may capitulate

The above values were directly programed into the event trees to improve clarity and avoid the construction of a large list of unique split fraction codes. Also, the following logic rules were used to determine the type and number of nuclear weapons used. This information is needed to answer the third question and make appropriate end state assignments.

- The USA never uses EMP weapons because of the collateral damage that would be experienced by U.S. allies.
- If strategic weapons are not used in the first strike or retaliation, then the conflict is presumed to end at that point without the use of strategic weapons.
- If strategic weapons are used in the retaliation strike, then the number of warheads exchanged is assumed to reach a total that equals at least the smaller stockpile size of the two adversaries.

3. Global cooling effects?

With the number of strategic weapons used in each scenario now known, this question asks if the scenario consequences include global cooling effects as described in Chapter 5.

The number of scenarios in each nuclear first strike event tree will vary depending on the responses to top event questions given by the above rules. An example event tree structure is shown below and the complete event trees for all initiators are shown in Appendix B.

Exhibit 14-13 Example Nuclear First Strike Event Tree

First Strike by	First strike weapons used?	Retaliation weapons used?	Global cooling effects?	#	End State
USA1	tactical	tactical (0)	GNo	1	twhd100
3.00E-03		EMP (.2)	GNo	2	swhd50+
		strategic (.2)	GC1	3	gcm
			No	4	swhd50
		none (.6)	GNo	5	twhd100

Chapter 15 - The MFRA2 Consequence Analysis

To complete the calculation of mega fatality risk we need to quantify, with uncertainty, consequences. Consequences for the MFRA2 are human fatalities but consequences can also be measured in injuries, other health effects, or damages as measured in dollars or other units. Consequences estimates are conditional, that is they only occur if the risk scenario takes place. Thus the arithmetic of the risk calculation and the units used to express risk are described by the following equations.

$$Frequency \times Prompt\ Fatalities = Risk$$

$$\frac{events}{unit\ of\ time} \times \frac{fatilities}{event} = \frac{fatilities}{unit\ of\ time}$$

For the MFRA, end state consequence categories were defined by estimating the size of the population affected and the fraction of this population that would die as a result of the events described in each scenario. To manage this process, I built a lethality matrix whose rows defined nine population ranges and the columns specified lethality fractions. The cells of the matrix then contained the resulting products of the mean population and lethality fraction at each intersection. I then selected cells from the matrix to represent the most likely and extreme values for each end state and used these values in *Crystal Ball* to build probability distribution for each end state. The distribution forms and values used were based on my judgement.

The data and analyses reported in this book now allow for more objective estimates of prompt fatality consequences to be made. The following exhibit lists the end state categories, the mean value of the estimated prompt fatalities and references to the bases for their values for each end state used in the MFRA2.

Exhibit 15-1 Prompt Fatality End States

End State Data		Mean Fatalities	Basis
Code	Description		
nomega	Not a mega fatality scenario		
PF10m	10 m asteroid impact on high population zone	1.2E+06	Chapter 14 analysis
pf100m	100 m impact asteroid impact	1.6E+07	Reference 4
chaos1	10 million affected by SLS failure	2.5E+06	Chapters 13 & 15
chaos2	100 million affected by SLS failure	2.5E+07	Chapters 13 & 15
chaos3	500 million affected by SLS failure	1.2E+08	Chapters 13 & 15
chaos4	2 billion affected by SLS failure	5.0E+08	Chapters 13 & 15
chaos5	7 billion affected by SLS failure	1.8E+09	Chapters 13 & 15
equake	direct fatalities + local chaos	2.6E+06	MFRA
flood	direct fatalities + local chaos	5.6E+06	MFRA
pand4	high severity w effective containment	9.7E+06	Chapter 15
pand5	high severity w/o effective containment	6.4E+07	Chapter 15
pand5p	high severity w/o effective containment + global SLS breakdown	1.2E+08	Chapter 15
nucattack	Low yield nuclear detonation	3.9E+05	Chapter 6 analysis
nucattackp	High yield nuclear detonation	6.6E+05	Chapter 6 analysis
cwdths	Mega fatality civil war	1.1E+06	Chapter 2 data
demodths	Mega fatality civil war + democide	1.9E+07	Chapter 2 data
iswardths	Mega fatality interstate war	1.7E+07	Chapter 2 data
twhd100	Nuc war w <100 tactical warheads used	5.8E+06	Chapter 6 analysis
twhd100+	Nuc war w <100 tactical warheads + EMP	1.5E+08	Chapter 6 analysis
twhd200	Nuc war w <200 tactical warheads	1.2E+07	Chapter 6 analysis
swhd10	Nuc war w <10 strategic warheads used	5.6E+06	Chapter 6 analysis
swhd50	Nuc war w <50 strategic warheads used	3.3E+07	Chapter 6 analysis
swhd50p	Nuc war w <50 strategic warheads + EMP	5.8E+07	Chapter 6 analysis
swhd120	Nuc war w 100 to 250 strategic warheads used	7.6E+07	Chapter 6 analysis
gcm	Global cooling moderate & nuc war w 250 to 500 strategic warheads used	8.3E+08	Chapter 6 analysis
gcs	Global cooling severe & nuc war w 1000 to 1750 strategic warheads used	3.2E+09	Chapter 6 analysis
gcc	Global cooling catastrophic & nuc war w >3000 strategic warheads used	5.8E+09	Chapter 6 analysis

Some of these end state categories deserve further explanation. The *chaos* family of end states is used to represent the consequences of long term electric power outages and other scenarios where societal life support systems (SLS) have broken down. Five categories in this family were defined for different population sizes that could be impacted. As I discussed earlier, I found no comprehensive work done to estimate the possible level of fatalities that would occur under loss of SLS conditions. But References 31 to 33 indicate that such estimates are presented for EMP events in classified reports and that they indicate that the lethality fraction may reach 60% or more. Based on this evidence, I used a lognormal distribution to represent the uncertainty for each chaos end state and set the mean lethality at 20% and the 95th percentile at 60%. This results in a very broad distribution for each category.

The pandemic end state categories were developed from the CDC pandemic severity index. This index characterizes the most severe category 5 flu pandemic as one that infects 30% of an exposed population and kills 2% of those infected. These percentages were used to set mean value fatalities for a regional population of one billion for end state *pand4* and the global population of seven billion for *pand5*. End state *pand5p* was used for a global pandemic so severe that its consequences were increased by a breakdown of societal life support systems. A doubling of the *pand5* fatality totals was allowed for this possibility.

Fatality distributions for high intensity conventional wars deaths were developed from the war death data in Chapter 2. By our definition, high intensity conflicts have at least one million fatalities. The historical average fatality level for multi-national wars was about 11 million, for civil wars it was about 1.3 million, and for civil wars with democide, about 28 million. High end fatalities for each war category were set at 50 million, 5 million, and 50 million respectively, and triangular distributions using these values were input to *Crystal Ball*.

The mean values of fatality distributions for the nuclear war end states were set using the guidelines from Exhibit 6-1. This was done by multiplying the number of warheads used by the appropriate factors from Exhibit 6-1. Uncertainty in these fatalities was represented with lognormal distributions by setting the 95th percentile values at two times the mean values.

For EMP only scenarios, the *chaos* end states discussed earlier were used to maintain consistency with the treatment of other loss of electric power scenarios.

The distributions for the three global cooling end states *gcm*, *gcs*, and *gcc* required special treatment. First, there are multiple initiating events that result in global cooling. These events are very different and cause fatalities in both direct (nuclear blast effects) and indirect (widespread crop failure) ways. Attempting to build these distributions by somehow combining these multiple effects could produce tails that included data points with more than 7.2 billion fatalities, which is not possible. As a result, the uncertainty in these distributions has to be carefully controlled and allowed to extend to the left or below the most likely values. Thus, to control the maximum and minimum values within credible ranges and still allow for large uncertainty, triangular distributions described in the following exhibit were used for these end states.

Exhibit 15-2 Global Cooling End State Distributions

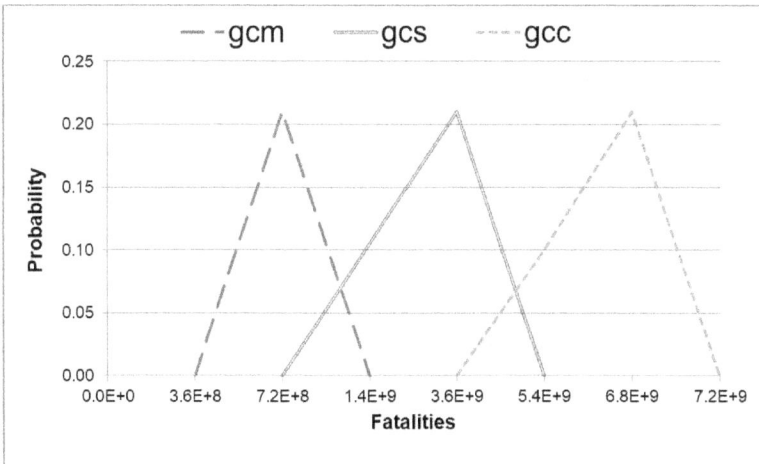

Chapter 16 - MFRA2 Results

Top Level Results

Let's first look at the total mega fatality risk predicted by the MFRA2 model. The next exhibit shows the probability distribution for mega fatality risk calculated in *Crystal Ball*.

Exhibit 16-1 Total Mega Fatality Risk

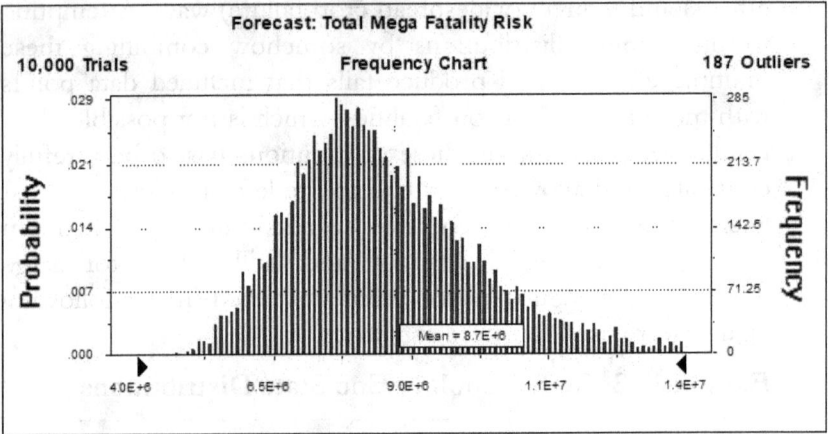

The mean value of this result is 8.65E6 prompt fatalities per year. This represents an individual risk of about 1.2E-3 per person per year for a global population of 7.2 billion. This result is only about 4% lower than the mean value of the original MFRA shown in Exhibit 1-3. We will explore the causes of this difference shortly, but first let's take a detailed look at the contributors to the MFRA2 results

Initiating Events

The exhibit below shows how the initiating events ranked in contribution to risk.

Exhibit 16-2 Contributions of Initiating Events to Risk

Initiator	Frequency (events/yr)	Risk (Fatalities per year)	Risk Rank (%)
Nuclear war in the Syria/Iraq conflict theater	3.3E-03	2.2E+06	25.0%
Conventional armed conflict	9.8E-02	1.1E+06	12.4%
Solar storms	3.7E-03	1.0E+06	11.9%
Nuclear war in the Crashwar conflict theater	3.3E-03	7.1E+05	8.2%
Biological accident	4.9E-02	6.3E+05	7.2%
Electric power system sabotage	1.4E-02	5.7E+05	6.5%
Naturally occurring pandemic	4.4E-02	5.6E+05	6.4%
Nuclear launch on false warning war	5.8E-04	4.9E+05	5.6%
Nuclear war in the Korea conflict theater	6.0E-03	4.4E+05	5.1%
Nuclear war in the East Europe conflict theater	3.3E-04	2.2E+05	2.5%
Nuclear war in the Ukraine conflict theater	3.3E-04	2.2E+05	2.5%

By grouping the initiating events into categories, we can get good picture of how the importance of these categories changed from the original MFRA results.

Exhibit 16-3 Comparison of MFRA 1&2 Results

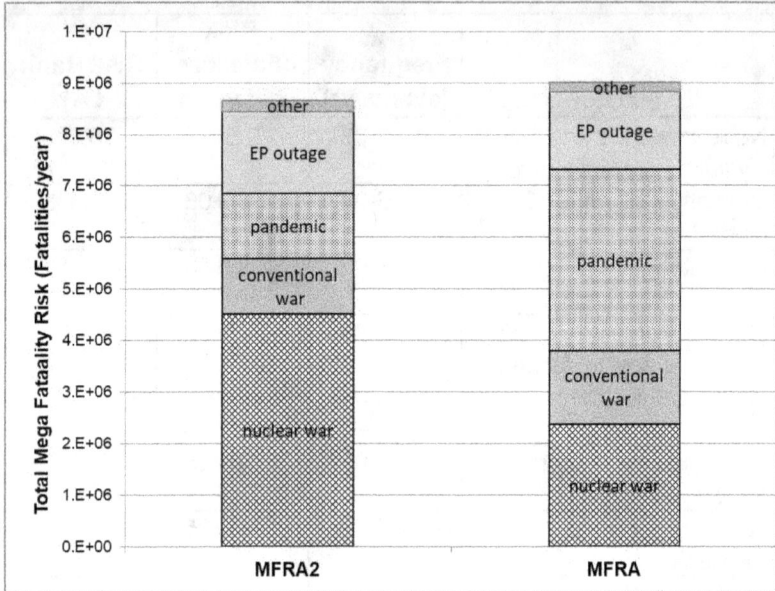

The impacts of the changes I discussed individually earlier can now be seen clearly. In summary, they are:

- Pandemic mega fatality risk was over stated in the MFRA because some lower intensity, non-mega fatality epidemics were included in the earlier results.

- Scenarios leading to less than mega fatality conventional war end states were also removed from the updated analysis, but this was more than offset by a dramatic increase in nuclear war risk.

- The overall likelihood of a nuclear war occurring estimated by each model was very consistent even though significantly different modeling approaches were used.

- Although the likelihood of nuclear war was estimated to be about the same in both models, the mega fatality risk of nuclear war risk was assessed to be much greater in the MFRA2 analysis because of the addition of "nuclear winter" global cooling effects into the MFRA2 consequence analysis.

One note of caution needs to be made for the electric power outage risk shown in Exhibit 16-3. This breakdown by initiating event category captures only electric power outage caused by solar storms and sabotage. Electric power outages caused by nuclear EMP weapons are included in the nuclear war category for this exhibit. I'll examine this issue more closely shortly.

End States

The next exhibit shows the risk ranking for each of the end states. Since each scenario terminates into a specific end state, the risk ranking here is just the percentage contribution of each end state to the total risk. This result also helps show where to focus risk reduction actions in order to produce the most effect on risk results.

Exhibit 16-4 End States Ranked by Contribution to Risk

End State	Representative Scenario	Risk (fatalities/yr)	Risk Rank
gcc	Nuclear war with catastrophic global cooling	2.3E+06	26.8%
pand4	High severity pandemic	8.8E+05	10.1%
gcm	Nuclear war or asteroid strike with moderate global cooling	8.5E+05	9.8%
twhd100p	Nuclear war with EMP & tactical weapons use	7.9E+05	9.2%
chaos3	Continent wide electric power system sabotage	5.5E+05	6.3%
demodths	Mega fatality civil war with democide	5.4E+05	6.2%
iswardths	Mega fatality interstate conventional war	4.9E+05	5.7%
gcs	Launch on false warning nuclear war	4.9E+05	5.7%
chaos4	Solar storm with hemispheric long term electric power outage	4.7E+05	5.4%
chaos5	Severe solar storm with global electric power outage	3.3E+05	3.8%

It is also instructive to group like end states into larger categories. In this higher level summary I am now able to gather all electric power outage risk together.

Exhibit 16-5 End State Categories

End State Category	Risk Rank
Nuclear war with global cooling	42.3%
Long term loss of electric power	28.0%
High severity pandemic	14.7%
Conventional war	12.4%
Other categories	2.6%

Scenario Level Results

Now let's look at the results for the individual scenarios. The next exhibit lists the top ten scenarios by contribution to total risk. Note that no initiating event shows up more than once in the top ten scenarios.

Exhibit 16-6 Scenarios Ranked by Contribution to Risk

Scenario #	Scenario Description	Risk (PF/yr)	Risk Rank (%)
USAfive3	USA - Russia nuclear war in Syria/Iraq conflict therater	1.8E+06	20.3%
armcon2	Mega fatality civil war with democide	5.4E+05	6.2%
USAsix3	USA - China nuclear war in the crashwar conflict theater	5.0E+05	5.7%
armcon1	Mega fatality interstate conventional war	4.9E+05	5.7%
lofw3	Launch on false warning USA - Russia nuclear war	4.7E+05	5.5%
SolStrm3	Solar storm with hemispheric electric power outage	4.7E+05	5.4%
bioaccident1	Bio lab accident causing a high severity pandemic with effective containment	4.6E+05	5.3%
Natepid1	Naturally occurring high severity pandemic with effective containment	4.1E+05	4.7%
NKorea1	N Korea - USA nuclear war in the Korea conflict theater	3.5E+05	4.0%
epsabotage4	Sabotage causing a continent wide electric power outage & SLS breakdown	3.3E+05	3.8%

The Importance of Electric Power Outages

I mentioned earlier that the normal views of the risk results don't completely capture the importance of long term electric power outages. This is because electric power outages can result from three very different sources; solar storms, direct system sabotage, and EMP nuclear weapon detonation. But EMP outages are not initiators in our risk model; they result from nuclear war initiators. Also, scenarios that include EMP weapons use can have other direct nuclear weapons effects as well. To improve our understanding of this important class of events I built the following graphics that break out the relative contributions of the three outage causes to the total likelihood of occurrence for extended electric power outages and for their total contribution to mega fatality risk.

Exhibit 16-7 Breakdown of EP Outage Frequency

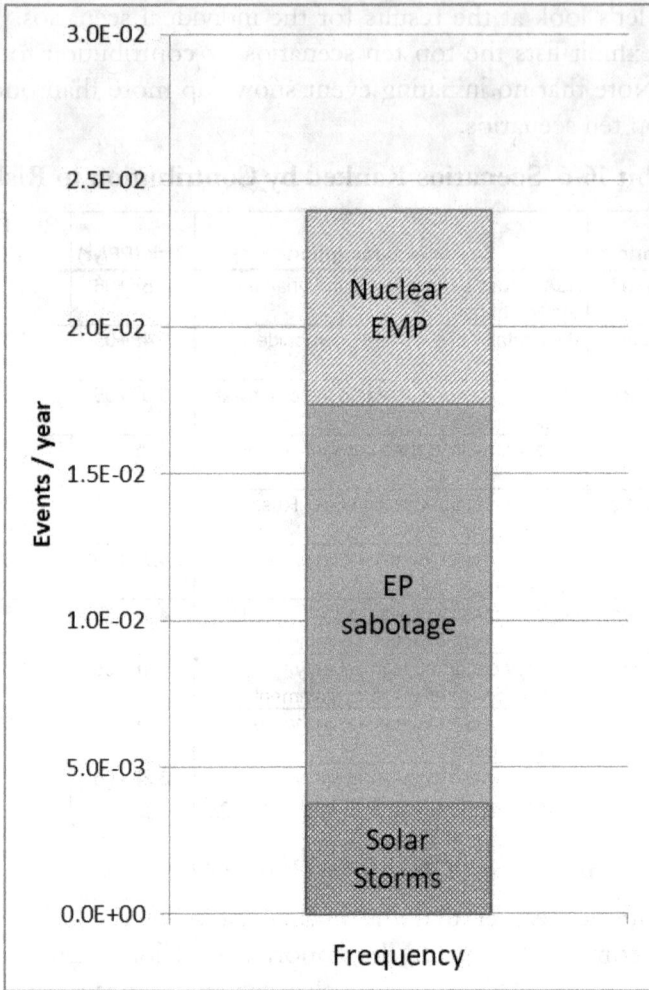

Exhibit 16-8 Breakdown of EP Outage Risk

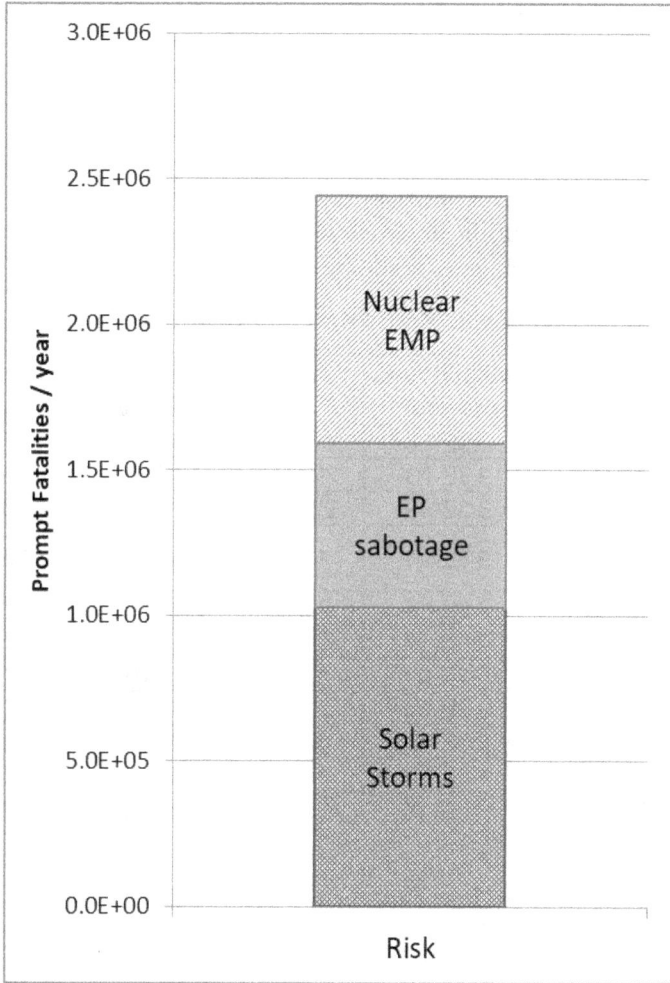

Note that the total mega fatality risk attributed to EP outages is now 2.4E6 or about 28% of total mega fatality risk. EP sabotage is the largest contributor to the likelihood of outages, but because sabotage outages were assessed to be less severe, risk is controlled more by solar storms and EMP.

A Closer Look at Nuclear War Risk

The structure of the MFRA2 mega fatality risk model allows the likelihood of nuclear war to be obtained straightforwardly by totaling the contributing initiating events (1.46E-2 per year) and the mega fatality risk to be seen by summing the mean values of the risk calculated for each nuclear war scenario (4.50E6 fatalities per year). This risk model structure also allows the contributors to both nuclear war likelihood and risk to be identified as can be seen in the next two exhibits.

Exhibit 16-9 Nuclear War Totals by Conflict Theater

Conflict Theater	Likelihood per year	% of Total	Risk (fatalities/yr)	% of Total
Korea	6.0E-03	41.0%	4.4E+05	9.8%
Crashwar	3.3E-03	22.6%	7.1E+05	15.8%
Syria/Iraq	3.3E-03	22.6%	2.2E+06	48.0%
Launch on False Warning	5.8E-04	4.0%	4.9E+05	10.8%
E Europe	3.3E-04	2.3%	2.2E+05	4.8%
Kashmir	3.3E-04	2.3%	1.7E+05	3.7%
Ukraine	3.3E-04	2.3%	2.2E+05	4.8%
S China Sea	3.3E-04	2.3%	7.1E+04	1.6%
Sikkim	6.0E-05	0.4%	3.0E+04	0.7%
Israel	6.0E-05	0.4%	4.6E+03	0.1%
	1.46E-02	100.0%	4.50E+06	100.0%

Exhibit 16-10 Nuclear War Totals by Nation

Nation	Likelihood per year	% of Total	Risk (fatalities/yr)	% of Total
USA*	1.02E-02	69.7%	3.39E+06	75.4%
N Korea	3.00E-03	20.5%	3.75E+05	8.3%
Russia*	6.52E-04	4.5%	4.99E+05	11.1%
China	3.60E-04	2.5%	4.80E+04	1.1%
Pakistan	3.00E-04	2.1%	1.50E+05	3.3%
India	6.00E-05	0.4%	3.01E+04	0.7%
Iran	3.00E-05	0.2%	2.29E+03	0.1%
Israel	3.00E-05	0.2%	2.29E+03	0.1%

(*) -includes 1/2 of launch on false warning risk

The first exhibit lists the contributors to nuclear war likelihood and mega fatality risk by conflict theater. Korea is projected to be the most likely source of a nuclear conflict but Syria/Iraq, crashwar, and launch on false warning were estimated to yield greater consequences and thus greater mega fatality risk.

The second exhibit lists the contributors to nuclear war likelihood and mega fatality risk by nation that initiates the first strike. Here the largest contributor is clearly the USA. This result stems from the high level of economic instability assessed in Chapter 12 and discussed further in the next section.

Although the above quantitative results may appear to be very definitive, remember that the basis for the allocation of first strike frequencies was based on qualitative analyses of first strike risk and nuclear state instability. Changes in these qualitative rankings would produce commensurate changes in conflict theater and nation risk rankings. Changes in the qualitative risk rankings would not, however, have a dramatic effect on the overall frequency of nuclear war and resulting level of mega fatality risk.

The Importance of American Debticide

In Chapter 12 I highlighted the increase in assessed USA nuclear first strike likelihood caused by economic instability in the United States. To measure how this impacted the overall MFRA2 results, the risk model was recalculated using the base case first strike frequencies from Exhibit 12-5. The next exhibit shows the difference in nuclear war attributable to U.S. economic instability.

Exhibit 16-11 Importance of Debticide

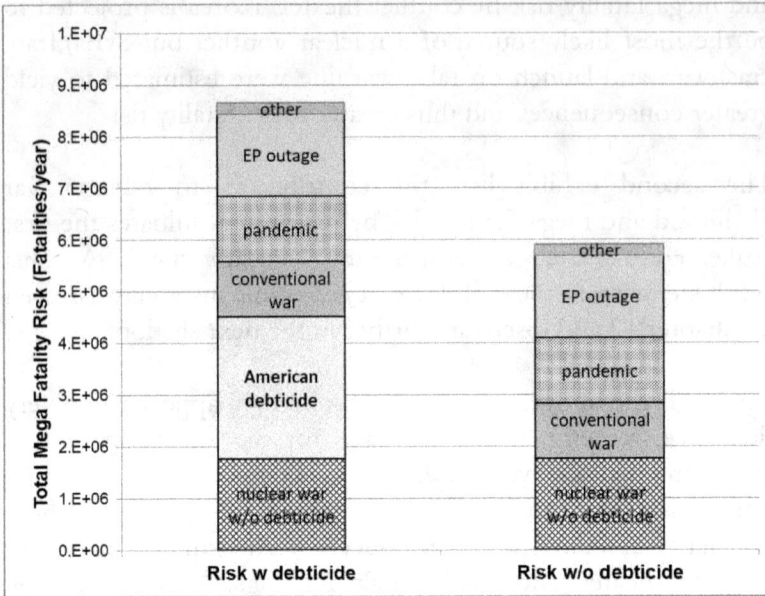

The nuclear state instability analysis results cause nuclear war risk to more than double and total mega fatality risk to increase by 47%. This means that about one third of the final total for mega fatality risk is attributable to American debticide.

Part VI - Of Risk and Men

Chapter 17 - What Else Could Kill Me?

If mega fatality events account for about 15% of total prompt fatality risk, then what makes up the other 85%? To provide an answer to this question we can consult the robust mortality data compiled by the World Health Organization (WHO). WHO compiles mortality records from all member countries on an annual basis. The WHO data indicates that the global aggregate death rate has been steadily decreasing for as long as global data has been available, although they note that the completeness and consistency of the data is best for the period since 2000. The latest year for which data is available is 2015 and I have assumed that a full year of data for global deaths is sufficiently representative of all recent years for the purpose of this analysis. WHO categorizes deaths by cause, sex, age, and location. Causes of death are binned into about 200 standardized categories and location is reported by country and WHO region (17-1). This is much more detail than needed for this analysis, so I condensed the data into the following nine cause of death categories.

1. Total from all causes
2. Noncommunicable diseases
3. Communicable diseases
4. Road injury
5. Other unintentional injuries
6. Self-harm
7. Interpersonal violence
8. Collective violence & War
9. Natural disasters

The WHO data on population and number of deaths for each category can be used to calculate the annual risk of death per person. In 2015, WHO recorded 56,441,320 deaths in a population of 7,344,362,389 resulting in a total aggregated annual individual death risk of 7.68E-3 per person. This aggregated average risk will of course vary depending on the age, sex, and location of each individual. Some causes of death will certainly vary by age and gender, but for this analysis, I thought it would be most important to know how much the risk for each cause category could vary by country. This is because one cannot change their sex or age in hope of controlling risk, but one can change their location. The following exhibits show how much the country with the highest risk varies from the average and how much the USA average differs from the global average.

Exhibit 17-1 WHO Data for Individual Death Risk

	USA	Global average	Lowest country	Highest country	
All Causes	8.3E-03	7.7E-03	1.0E-03	1.6E-02	Ukraine
Noncommunicable diseases	7.3E-03	5.4E-03	6.8E-04	1.5E-02	Somalia
Communicable diseases	4.5E-04	1.6E-03	1.3E-04	8.7E-03	Ukraine
Road injury	1.1E-04	1.8E-04	2.9E-05	4.6E-04	Zimbabwe
Other unintentional injuries	2.1E-04	3.0E-04	5.1E-05	9.2E-04	Angola
Self-harm	1.4E-04	1.1E-04	1.4E-05	3.7E-04	Sri Lanka
Interpersonal violence	5.3E-05	6.4E-05	3.2E-06	8.6E-04	Honduras
Collective violence & War	1.2E-07	2.1E-05	0.0E+00	3.3E-03	Syria
Natural disasters	1.6E-06	1.9E-06	0.0E+00	3.3E-04	Nepal

Exhibit 17-2 Death Risk for Disease

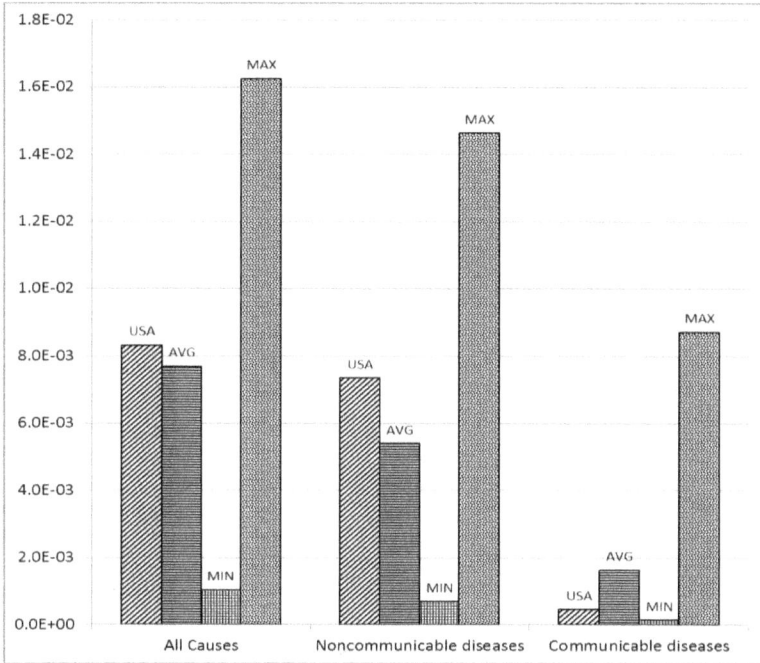

Exhibit 17-3 Death Risk for Injuries

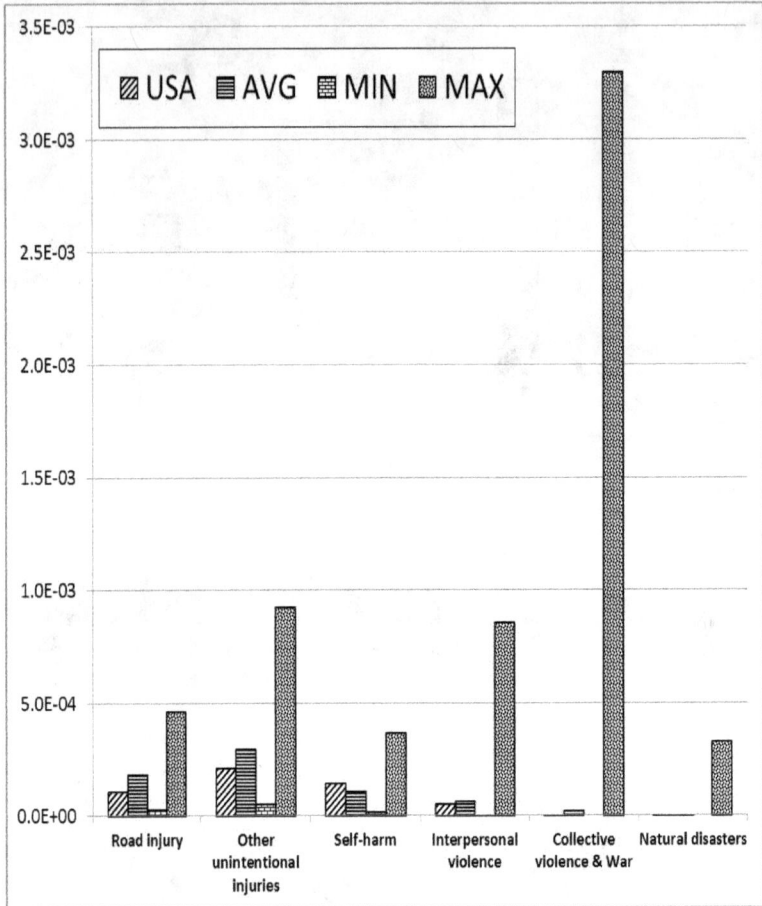

Just examining the raw data from WHO in the above exhibits provides some interesting insights.

- The USA ranks somewhat above average for noncommunicable diseases but somewhat below average for communicable diseases. This may stem from the politically correct labeling of alcohol & drug abuse deaths as being from a noncommunicable "disease" rather than self-harm.
- Despite HIV/AIDS and Ebola being so prevalent in central Africa, the nation with the highest communicable disease death risk was Ukraine.

- I was surprised that road injuries or auto accidents did not vary more. The nation with the highest accident risk, Zimbabwe, was only about double the global average.
- Interpersonal violence does vary significantly among countries with the highest risk nation, Honduras, having a murder risk more than ten times higher than the global average. Other nations in central and South America also exhibited elevated murder rates.
- Death risk from collective violence or war showed extreme differences between nations. While many nations reported zero or near zero risk in this category, the ongoing civil war in Syria resulted in 3.3 deaths per thousand people in 2015. This death risk is more than **100 times higher** than the global average and more than **25,000 times higher** than the level of this risk in the USA and other stable nations. It is no wonder that a mass migration of people away from this area is taking place.
- Natural disaster death risk also varies significantly with only a few nations reporting any deaths at all in 2015. The normal or background risk for natural disasters is so low that any significant event, even one well below the mega fatality level, will produce a notable bump in the annual WHO data.

To complete the answer to this chapter's question, however, we have one more task to perform. Because no significant mega fatality events occurred in 2015, the WHO data does not fully account for this element of death risk. To complete the death risk profile we must add mega fatality risk to the random individual risk statistics reported for 2015. The MFRA results reported in RMR Chapter 16 indicate that mega fatality events will add about 15% to the total individual risk. But with the updated mega fatality risk estimates from Part V and the random individual death risk data categorized in this chapter, we can now perform this addition more comprehensively. I did this by reviewing the scenario level MFRA2 results and assigning each scenario to a WHO cause of death category. This was very straightforward for most scenarios, but not all.

Disease deaths from pandemics that were deliberately initiated as acts of terrorism or war were assigned to *collective violence & war* rather than to *communicable disease*. Also deaths resulting from extended electric power system outages were assigned based on the nature of the initiator. Those caused by solar storms were assigned to *natural disasters* while those caused by sabotage or nuclear EMP detonation were binned to *collective violence & war*.

Because all the mega fatality risks bin down into only three of the WHO cause of death categories: communicable diseases, collective violence & war, and natural disasters, we are going to simplify the data shown earlier by combining all unintentional injuries into one category. The following exhibit then shows the results of this simplification and the summation of random individual and mega fatality risk to produce total individual death risk.

Exhibit 17-4 Combined Total Death Risk by Category

Cause of Death	Random Individual Risk	Mega Fatality Individual Risk	Total Individual Death Risk
All Causes	7.68E-03	1.20E-03	8.88E-03
Noncommunicable diseases	5.38E-03	0.00E+00	5.38E-03
Communicable diseases	1.63E-03	1.77E-04	1.81E-03
All unintentional injuries	6.49E-04	0.00E+00	6.49E-04
Collective violence & War	2.13E-05	8.53E-04	8.75E-04
Natural disasters	1.92E-06	1.71E-04	1.73E-04

Now let's recast this table to show the relative percentage of total risk in each category from both random and mega fatality events.

Exhibit 17-5 Random & Mega Fatality % Contributions

Cause of Death	Random Individual Risk	Mega Fatality Individual Risk	Total Individual Death Risk
All Causes	86%	14%	100%
Noncommunicable diseases	100%	0%	100%
Communicable diseases	90%	10%	100%
Other unintentional injuries	100%	0%	100%
Collective violence & War	2%	98%	100%
Natural disasters	1%	99%	100%

Observe that the overall contribution of 13.5% to total fatality risk fails to communicate the more interesting story. Mega fatality pandemics represent about 10% of the total risk from communicable disease. Only when a communicable disease breaks out above the long term chronic level does it become a pandemic. War and natural disasters, however, exhibit a starkly different pattern. These causes of death categories are almost completely dominated by mega fatality risk. In these categories, the normal background level of risk is almost nonexistent. This is certainly not the intuitive result many might expect. News media coverage of anyone unfortunate enough to die in a tornado, flood, earthquake, hurricane, or other natural event is extensive. But these events, dramatic as they are, do not produce a large enough number of fatalities during a typical year to register as a significant risk contributor. Even an exceptional event like the Tohoku earthquake and tsunami would only raise global natural disaster risk to about 4% of individual risk, if it had occurred in 2015. Per the WHO data, war deaths do occur on a consistent but low level with specific hot spots, like Syria, being significantly affected. This background risk is dwarfed by what could happen.

To further illustrate these results, here are pie charts showing the percentage contributions of each death risk category. The first exhibit shows only random individual risk while the second shows the percentage contributions with random individual and mega fatality risk combined.

Exhibit 17-6 Percent Contributions to Random Risk

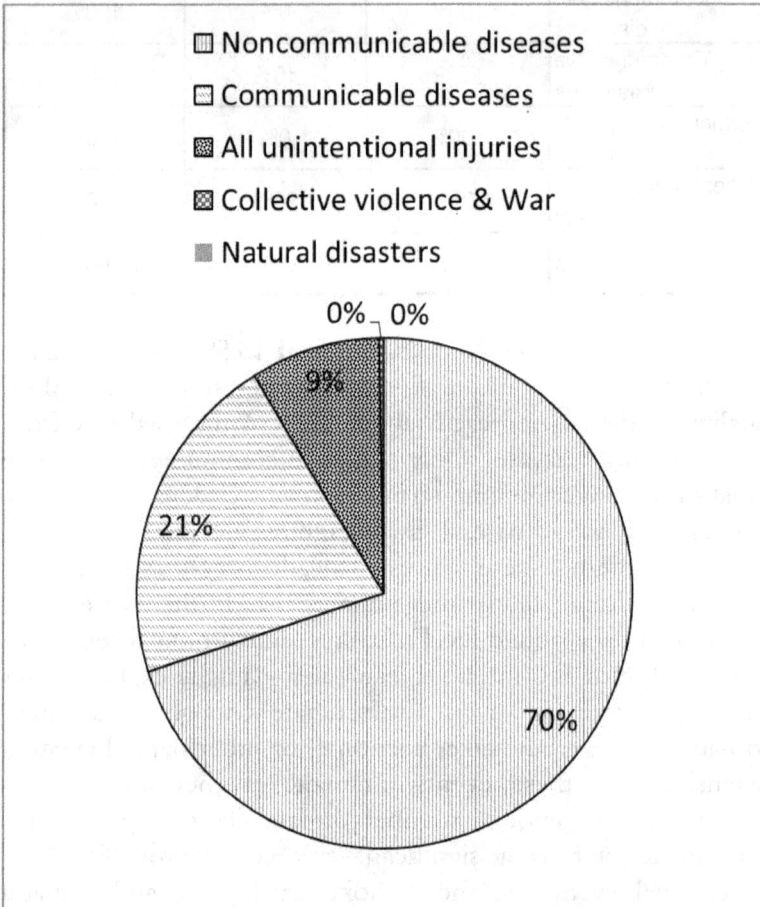

Legend:
- Noncommunicable diseases
- Communicable diseases
- All unintentional injuries
- Collective violence & War
- Natural disasters

0% 0%
9%
21%
70%

Exhibit 17-7 Percent Contributions to Total Risk

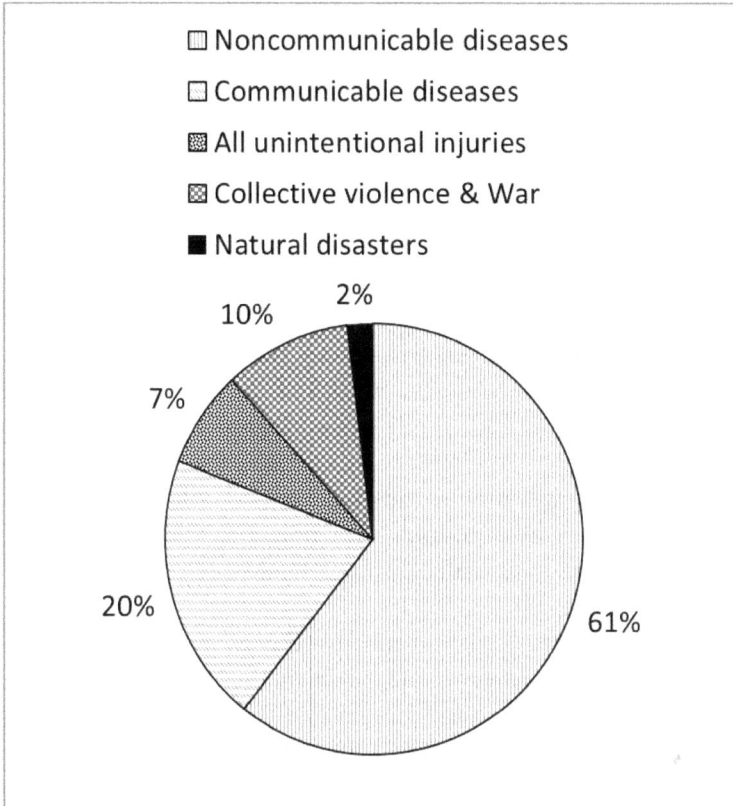

- ▥ Noncommunicable diseases
- ▫ Communicable diseases
- ▦ All unintentional injuries
- ▨ Collective violence & War
- ■ Natural disasters

2%
10%
7%
20%
61%

Chapter 17 References:

17-1.　Global Health Estimates 2015: Deaths by Cause, Age, Sex, by Country and by Region, 2000-2015. Geneva, World Health Organization; 2016.

Chapter 18 - Perspectives on Death Risk

Now that we have compiled the data and answered our first question, we can now ask if mega fatality events represent a risk that anyone should care about.

Individual Risk

An individual perspective on death risk can be viewed directly from the data in Chapter 2. On a global average basis, mega fatality risk (MFR) represents about 13.5% of the average person's total death risk or 1.2 E-3 per year. This is a big enough number to capture the attention of many if not most people. But, whether you stay awake at night worrying about this stealthy 13.5% add-on to your risk profile or not will depend on your personal sensitivity or tolerance for risk. In the next chapter, we will discuss this further and will look to see if there are any possible actions that may be able to reduce a specific individual's exposure to mega fatality events.

But before that, let's look for another way to gain some insight onto how important mega fatality risk might be. To do this we can look back at the data in Chapter 2 and ask how this level of risk compares with the potential increase in risk that a person would experience by living in a maximum risk country instead of an average risk country. The following exhibit presents this calculation and compares the results for each cause of death category with mega fatality risk.

Exhibit 18-1 Location Risk Differences vs MFR

	Global average	Highest country	Difference	% of MFR
All Causes	7.7E-03	1.6E-02	8.5E-03	697%
Noncommunicable diseases	5.4E-03	1.5E-02	9.2E-03	754%
Communicable diseases	1.6E-03	8.7E-03	7.1E-03	577%
Road injury	1.8E-04	4.6E-04	2.8E-04	23%
Other unintentional injuries	3.0E-04	9.2E-04	6.3E-04	51%
Self-harm	1.1E-04	3.7E-04	2.6E-04	21%
Interpersonal violence	6.4E-05	8.6E-04	7.9E-04	65%
Collective violence & War	2.1E-05	3.3E-03	3.3E-03	267%
Natural disasters	1.9E-06	3.3E-04	3.3E-04	27%

The above table clearly tells us that the individual death risk spread between the average and maximum risk countries is much greater than the mega fatality risk across many cause categories. When totaled across all causes, the average to maximum risk spread is about a factor of seven greater than mega fatality risk. So, if an individual in a high risk country wanted to reduce their death risk exposure, their first priority should be to get the hell out of Dodge.

Family Risk

If the magnitude of mega fatality death risk for you as individual is not enough to get your attention, there may be another perspective on death risk that will. Let's say that in addition to caring about yourself, you also care about the death risk faced by your family or other group of people that is significant in your life. All the numbers we have used so far are aggregate fatality rates for death per person per year. That is the numbers give the likelihood of an individual dying from a specific cause or all causes on an annual basis. But now let's ask what the likelihood is that two people die in the same year.

If we know nothing about the two people and presume that their deaths are independent events, then we can use the following equation to calculate the likelihood of both persons dying in the same year.

$$TFR_n = IFR^n$$
$$TFR_2 = (8.9E - 3)^2$$
$$TFR_2 = 7.9E - 5$$

In this case, (TFR_n) is the total fatality risk of (n) deaths in one year and IFR is the independent fatality risk for one person from Exhibit 17-4 (8.9E-3) and (n), the number of multiple independent deaths or events, is 2.

But now let's sharpen our initial question and ask what the likelihood of death in the same year is if both persons are from the same family and that they live together. Is it still valid to assume that their deaths would be independent events? Perhaps not. There are numerous scenarios that could claim the lives of multiple family members at one time. Examples would include auto accidents, normal levels of contagious diseases, and tornados. And then there is the possible special impact of mega fatality events that could kill a large number of people in the area impacted by a mega fatality event. In other words, if one family member dies and the cause is known, there are multiple conditions where it would not be appropriate to use the random independent fatality rate to assess the likelihood of a second family member also dying.

As a primer for answering this question, I now ask you go back to *Risk Management Revisited (RMR)* and read the section of Chapter 12 titled *Combinatorial Errors and Dependence*. This subject is important here because we now have to examine the possible dependence between the deaths of these two people.

As a brief reminder, two events are said to be statistically independent when the actual occurrence of either event has no effect on the likelihood of the other event also occurring. Coin tosses, with a fair coin, are the classic example of independent events. When knowledge of the outcome of an event does change our assessment of the likelihood of the second event, these events are said to be dependent. The dependency can be strong, meaning that knowledge of one event gives us perfect knowledge of the other outcome or, the dependency can be weak with knowledge of one outcome only giving us partial knowledge of the second event. As I discussed in *RMR*, getting the assessment of dependencies right is critically important to the risk assessment process.

So how can the likelihood of two people dying in the same year be calculated considering the contributions of both independent events and dependent mega fatality events? Looking back at Exhibit 17-4, note that the total fatality risk for one person (TFR_1) is the sum of the WHO aggregated risk from all causes (IFR = 7.7E-3) and the mean mega fatality risk from the MFRA (MFR = 1.2E-3). As discussed in Chapter 15, the mega fatality risk is an aggregated sum of scenario level risks that are the product of the scenario frequency for the mega fatality event and the conditional end state consequences. The end state consequences are in turn the product of the estimated population impacted by the event and the fraction of that population that die. The total mega fatalities calculated are then divided by the global population to get the mean mega fatality risk. If, however, we know that the first family member did die from a mega fatality event, then we also know that the family is within the area impacted by the mega fatality event. With this added knowledge, we must now set the likelihood that the second family member also dies to the value of the lethality fraction used for that end state. In equation format:

$$TFR_n = IFR^n + (MFR \times LF^{n-1})$$

Since the lethality fractions (LF) are assigned and used at the scenario level, we don't know its precise value at the aggregate result level. But for this exercise, let's assign it a conservative value of 0.05 or one in twenty. Substituting this and the other values into the above equation, we now get:

$$TFR_2 = (7.7E - 3)^2 + ((1.2E - 3) \times (0.05)^{2-1})$$
$$TFR_2 = (5.9E - 5) + (6.1E - 5)$$
$$TFR_2 = 1.2E - 4$$

So, accounting for the possible dependence in the mega fatality risk caused our assessment of risk for a family of two to increase from 7.9E-5 to 1.2E-4, or an increase of 51%. If we increase the family size to three or four, the spread is even more dramatic as shown in next exhibit.

Exhibit 18-2 Mega Fatality Risk vs Family Size

Number of Family Members	Random Fatality Risk	Mega Fatality Risk	Total Family Risk	Mega Fatality % of Risk
1	7.68E-03	1.23E-03	8.91E-03	14%
2	5.90E-05	6.13E-05	1.20E-04	51%
3	4.53E-07	3.06E-06	3.52E-06	87%
4	3.48E-09	1.53E-07	1.57E-07	98%
LF= 0.05				

And, for lethality fractions other than 0.05, the results change as follows.

Exhibit 18-3 Sensitivity of Risk to Lethality Fraction

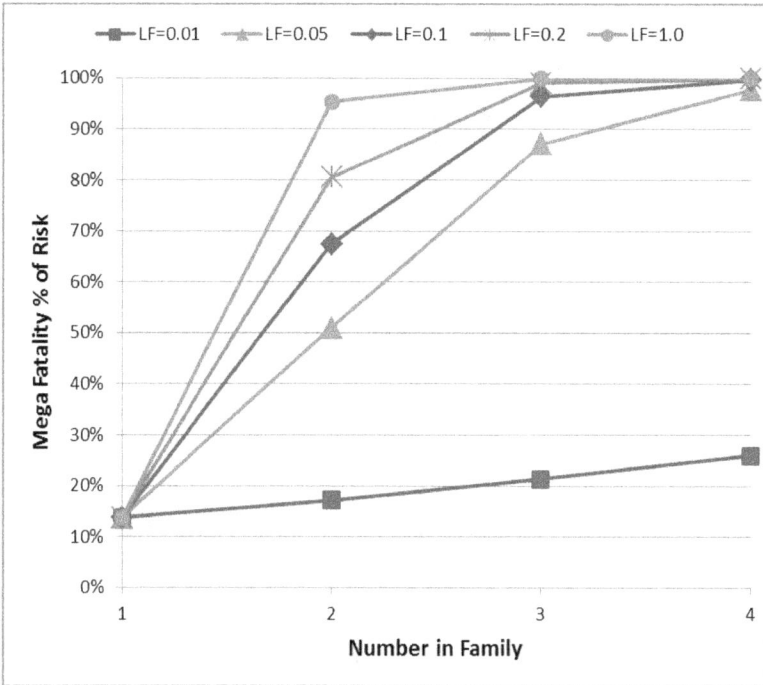

Risk Perspectives

The above analyses indicate that both individual and family risk exhibit strong spatial dependency. If you are an individual, it is very advisable to stay away from areas where death from any identifiable cause is significantly above global averages. This may be a very obvious finding, but many may be surprised at how strong this principle remains in the 21st century. It looks like the specter of the American Wild West is actually still with us.

Mega fatality risks proved to be especially important to family risk. Being within the area affected by a mega fatality event dramatically changes risk. The results here make sense both mathematically and intuitively. The higher the lethality fraction is with the affected zone, the more important it is to not be there. Exhibit 18-3 clearly illustrates the power of this spatial dependency. This exhibit also shows that as the lethality fraction for a mega fatality event becomes lower, it more closely resembles normal background risk. This conclusion is supported by the CDC's Pandemic Severity Index which begins at a case fatality ratio of 0.1%, which equals a lethality fraction of 0.001.

This influence of spatial dependence is further illustrated by the following exhibit. In this graphic, ten binary events (0 or 1) have occurred within a grid of 100 possible events. The mean likelihood of the event occurring is 10/100 or 0.1. Because the pattern of events appears random, we can validly say that the events appear to be independent and that knowledge of an event in a specific position gives us no new information about the probability of an event in any other position.

Exhibit 18-4 Random Independent Event Pattern

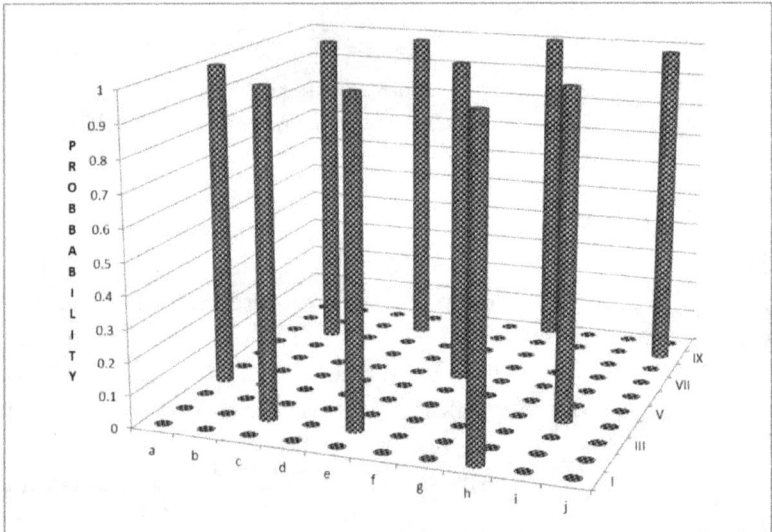

This knowledge shift is illustrated in the next exhibit. Pictured here is the same 10 x 10 grid with 10 binary events having occurred. However, the pattern of events this time is definitely not random. In this case, knowledge that an event has occurred in a specific position increases our assessment of the probability of an event in an adjacent position. The aggregate mean of event occurrence over the whole grid though is still 0.1.

Exhibit 18-5 Clustered Dependent Event Pattern

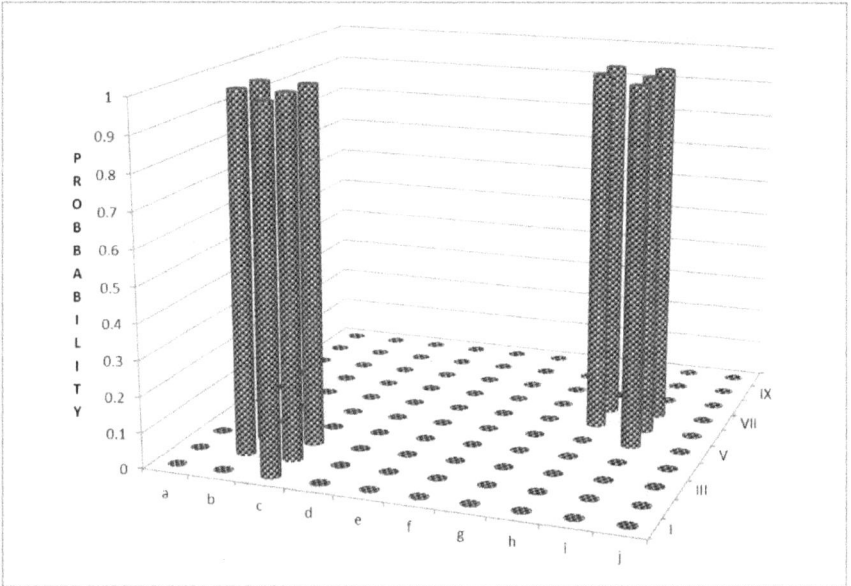

Chapter 19 - Building Your Personal Risk Profile

Let's now sum up what we have learned so far.

- On a global aggregate level, mega fatality risks add about 13.5% to the annual random mortality risk we each face.

- When broken down by cause of death, some categories show dramatic variations by location.

- Death risk from collective violence/war and natural disasters are dominated by mega fatality events.

- The annual death risk for a family or group greater than two is dominated by mega fatality events rather than random individual events.

Based on these findings, it would be logical for anyone to wonder where they and their family might stand within the wide spectrum of risk described so far. And, the immediate follow-on to that question would be: Is there anything that can be done to reduce my and my family's exposure to fatality risk?

To answer these questions I have composed a survey that you can answer based on your own personal circumstances to build your own personal risk profile. They are listed in the next exhibit. The answers shown reflect my personal risk profile. To see what your personal score is, you can download the *Personal Risk Profile Questionnaire* from my website at **jpkindinger.com** and answer the questions based on your own personal circumstances by selecting the letter representing your best answer for each question and placing it in the "answer" box. Your individual fatality risk and comparison to the average individual will automatically be calculated.

Survival Games

Exhibit 19-1 The Personal Risk Profile Questionnaire

Personal Risk Profile
(Place the letter of the appropriate answer in each box)

Questions	Answers
1) My age is?	D
A) < 30 years	
B) 30-49 years	
C) 50-59 years	
D) 60-69 years	
E) > 70 years	
2) The overall capability of my health care system is?	D
A) Significantly below average	
B) Somewhat below average	
C) About average	
D) Somewhat above average	
E) Significantly above average	
3) The level of personal violence where I live is?	A
A) Significantly below average	
B) Somewhat below average	
C) About average	
D) Somewhat above average	
E) Significantly above average	
4) The likelihood of life threatening natural disasters in the area where I live is?	B
A) Significantly below average	
B) Somewhat below average	
C) About average	
D) Somewhat above average	
E) Significantly above average	
5) How long could you live normally without electric power?	B
A) Only a few days	
B) A while, my water & septic systems don't need the grid	
C) Indefinitely, I live off the grid	
6) Do you live in an active war zone?	N
Y) Yes	
N) No	
7) Do you live in a nuclear weapons state?	Y
Y) Yes	
N) No	
8) Do you live in a tropical climate?	N
Y) Yes	
N) No	

Your personal annual fatality risk is:	1.48E-02
Your risk compared to the average individual risk is:	166.5%
Your personal non-age related annual fatality risk is:	2.66E-03
Your non-age related risk compared to the average individual is:	75.9%

Now let's walk through these questions and see what one might do to manage their risk.

1. Your age - Well after all this analysis it turns out that your biggest mortality risk factor is still your age. I could advise not getting old, but that strategy has some real drawbacks. If you refuse to answer this question in the survey, the default answer is "E" > 70 years, so you have to fess up. To provide some encouragement for us older folks, I also built the questionnaire to provide your personal risk score without the age-related component so that you can see the potential benefits of good overall risk management practices.

2. Health care – The availability of quality health care is an obviously important risk factor. The numbers added or subtracted from your baseline risk in this question reflect the variability of health care quality among nations. All nations are assumed to be equally vulnerable to the high severity pandemics included in the MFRA2 risk results. The recommended risk reduction strategy here is obvious, get access to the best quality health care you can. I also recognize that many people have little control over their access to health care.

3. Personal violence – Finally, we have a risk factor you can really do something about. The numbers added to your baseline risk in this question reflect the variability in violence among nations. This does not include the violence associated with open warfare, this will come later. The recommended risk reduction strategy here is to vote with your feet and get away from violent places and people. And, we see this strategy being exercised routinely by people leaving places like Central America and high crime areas of U.S. cities.

4. Natural disasters – The only natural hazard that made a large contribution to mega fatality risk on a global scale was solar storms. Everyone should be aware of their potential danger and I'll say more about this shortly. While other natural hazards may not be an important risk contributor

globally, they may be a very important contributor to risk in your local area and be a part of your personal risk profile. I grew up in the American Midwest where the summer weather is constantly monitored for tornados and where everyone has some form of shelter to go to if one appears. Other regions present different natural hazards, but the attention paid to risk management of these events is quite universal. This said, one can never plan for all contingencies, so when natural disasters do cause loss of life they get enormous attention. As a result, the recommended risk reduction action here is to pay attention to the hazards that can affect your area and have a plan of action for what to do if they happen. The only time I saw this advice ignored was while I was living in Orange County California. Following a large earthquake somewhere in the Pacific, a tsunami warning was issued for the California coast. Suddenly, the roads were jammed with surfers headed to the beach to catch the big wave! What more can I say?

5. Loss of electric power – This is an event I urge everyone to consider carefully. The more I research this event, the more convinced I become of the danger it poses. Solar storms are especially worrisome because of the vast scope of damage that is possible. A solar storm is capable of destroying a large swath of everything electrical or electronic across an entire continent. No electricity, no TV, no radio, no phones, no computers, no satellites. Without these electrical and electronic systems that we take for granted, vital societal life support systems will grind to a halt. Maintaining civil order will be a challenge. Within hours of the outage, the stress of exposure, dehydration, starvation, disease, and violence will begin to appear. This is the event that could prove the paranoid survivalists to be right. The recommended risk reduction strategy for loss of electric power events then has at least two elements. First, make an objective evaluation of your dependence on electric power and how long you can live without it. Can my family and I reliably get home if we are at work or school? Will your water supply and sanitary sewer systems work? How long

will my normal stores of food, water, and medicine last? Will my heating/cooling system work? The U.S. EMP Commission actually tested the effect of an EMP event on cars and found that most would survive okay because of the natural shielding provided by a steel body, but the engine might stall and need to be re-fired. Caution is needed in relying on these test results, however, since the newest of the cars tested were 2002 models that did not have the much more advanced electronic systems built into later models. So, your car may work but if the entire country is affected, where will you go? With the task of understanding your vulnerability to loss of power events done, you can then develop a strategy for survival. This is a big task that is beyond the scope of this book. Many other very specific books, guides, and checklists are available to help with the details of survival planning, and I'm not going to add another to the fray. Very shortly I will, however, try to bridge the gap between this book and a detailed survival plan. The idea of planning for an electric power outage might seem overwhelming, but don't use that as an excuse for inaction. Even if you conclude that you are extremely vulnerable and unable to weather a long outage, planning for even a modest outage could save the day if you experience a lesser magnitude outage.

6. <u>Live in a war zone?</u> – This is a pretty obvious fatality risk and one with an obvious risk reduction action that can be taken – to "get out of Dodge" as we say in America. Today millions from Ukraine, Libya, Iraq, and especially Syria are trying to do just that.

7. <u>Live in a nuclear weapons state</u>? – If your answer to this question is "yes", your government has developed and deployed nuclear weapons for the purpose of deterring aggression by adversaries. While this may be true and you currently benefit from the security provided by these weapons, they also make your nation, and you, a potential target if nuclear war should ever breakout. As a result, you bear an added risk factor that those in non-nuclear weapons states do not. Most people readily accept this risk, but if you

elect not to, you can relocate to a nuclear weapons free country. Such relocation will not protect you, however, from the risk discussed under the next question.

8. Tropical Living – Over 40% of the total mega fatality risk came from nuclear war and other events that caused global cooling. Those that live in tropical climates or can evacuate to tropical areas before the global cooling event becomes fully realized should have a better chance of survival. This is especially true for the scenarios that produced less than catastrophic global cooling.

So how did you do on this quiz? This is only a very short test that is really meant just to get you thinking about risk on a personal level. If I was successful, you now have at least a mental list of hazards that might deserve some attention in order to be avoided. So what can be done to reduce your fatality risk? This will be our final question.

Chapter 20 - Risk Management Strategies

To complete this journey, I want to present some guidance on how to develop a personal risk management strategy. As I said earlier, I will not be presenting another survivalist guide. But after gaining an understanding of both your individual and mega fatality risk contributors, you are now equipped to objectively consider the risk reduction strategies that might be practical and effective for you. I discussed many of these available actions individually in the previous paragraphs but a holistic approach to this question may reveal doable actions that yield benefits for multiple hazards.

First, after completing your personal risk profile, identify the hazards that are present for your specific location and circumstances. Next, objectively assess your ability and the ability of your family to respond to these hazards. The basic strategies for responding to danger start with the well-known decision of "fight or flight". In the context of fatality risk this better stated as "run or take shelter". In order to be successful, both basic strategies require planning and preparation.

Preparations for evacuation may vary from impromptu to very elaborate and complex. For example, warning of an approaching hurricane is available several days in advance and evacuation requires only getting in a car and driving away from the predicted path of the storm. In contrast, people living in nations with unstable or autocratic governments may make elaborate plans to escape a pending civil war or democidal political purge. These plans might include transferring money to another nation, sending children to school in another nation, purchasing real estate in another nation, obtaining dual citizenship, and arranging for emergency transportation over the border.

If no advance warning is available, it still may be possible to evacuate to safety after an event, if you can survive the immediate consequences. An example of this is strategy is once again the tornado. If you live in an area prone to tornados, you can expect only a few minutes warning, if any, that the storm is coming. As a result, you must have at least a small shelter from the storm readily available that can protect you for a few minutes during the passage of the storm. Even if your home and the immediate neighborhood are completely destroyed, you can walk to safety afterward if your storm shelter held fast. This could be called a hybrid shelter-evacuate strategy. Other hazards may offer more warning time, or none at all, and may be more, or less, survivable. You will need to make this assessment based on known local conditions.

If sheltering is the selected strategy, the family or other persons desiring protection must arrive before falling victim to the hazard that is about to or has already occurred. For hazards that afford little or no warning, a prepared action plan for what to do if the family is dispersed away from the shelter and normal transportation and/or communications are cut off may be critical to survival.

Assuming the shelter is reached in a timely manner, it must then be able to protect its occupants against the threatening hazard. Depending on the level of protection desired, preparing a shelter for high risk events may be a quite complex task. To help in selecting a successful and practical shelter design, I will discuss several attributes to consider in planning for and preparing a shelter and then I'll run a test of the ability of several general types of shelters to provide for survival against high risk hazards.

Survival Shelter Attributes

Hazard protection
The first function of any shelter is to protect its occupants from the immediate effects of hazardous conditions. Normal housing construction has evolved over time to provide substantial protections from common hazards and is often enhanced to address local hazards. For example, Midwestern American homes may have basements or storm shelters for tornado protection, California homes are typically strengthened to resist earthquake motion, and coastal Florida homes are built on stilts

to protect against hurricane flooding. Normal housing construction features may not be adequate, however, to deal with the hazards presented by mega fatality events so let's look deeper. Here is a simple rating system you can use to assess your current state of readiness for surviving the immediate effects of high risk hazards.

Exhibit 20-1   Shelter Immediate Hazard Protection Ratings

Shelter immediate hazard protection capability	Shelter hazard protection rating
Structural vulnerability increases risk to occupants	H0
Structure provides no significant hazard protection to occupants	H1
Structure provides reasonable protection from relevant hazards	H2
Structure provides robust protection from relevant hazards	H3

In assigning these shelter ratings, the relative location of the shelter with respect to the hazard must be considered. For example, in an area expected to be targeted by nuclear weapons during a conflict, a shelter would have to be deeply buried and heavily reinforced to provide any measure of protection from nuclear blast effects. But many miles away from the target area, blast effects would not be high on the risk list. An example of a H0 shelter would be an unreinforced stone or masonry structure in an earthquake zone. In this case occupants actually need to flee the shelter to improve their immediate safety.

Exposure protection
Normal housing uses external energy inputs and keeps its occupants comfortable and protected from the weather typical of its location. Global cooling events are the highest rated mega fatality events in the MFRA2. I listed earlier what the expected effects of moderate, severe, and catastrophic global cooling events would be on average temperatures, but those affected

will also have to survive periods of extreme cold temperatures, especially in the first winter season after the initiating event. These temperature extremes will obviously be lower than the averages indicate. The exhibit below indicates how much colder I estimate the extreme temperatures will be than the lowest temperature that has been experienced in a specific location before the global cooling event. The exposure ratings indicate that the shelter can protect its occupants from freezing under these temperature extremes without external energy inputs.

Exhibit 20-2 Shelter Exposure Ratings

Global cooling severity	Drop below normal low temperature (°F)	Shelter exposure rating
none	0	E0
moderate	-10 to -20	E1
severe	-25 to -35	E2
catastrophic	-40 to -50	E3

Thus, if the normally experienced low in your area is 50°F and we suffer a moderate global cooling event, a shelter needs to protect you from a 40 or 30 degree cold spell – no big deal. But, 40 or 50 degrees below normal lows will be a challenge for almost everyone. As a result, these shelter ratings are relative to the climate zone they are in. An E3 shelter in a tropical location might be fairly easy to build, but an E3 in Canada would need to be a very robust facility, probably a mine shaft or buried bunker.

Beyond global cooling events, exposure may be a problem for loss of electric power events in northern climates. Here normal housing structures may not be able to protect their occupants from normal low temperatures without external energy supplies. An objective assessment of your current housing may indicate that it fails to achieve even an E0 rating.

Water supply

A clean and reliable water supply is essential to human survival for both short and long term events. Bottled water can suffice for short durations but for the long term a fresh water supply from the environment or a reliable purification system is needed. Virtually all urban and suburban homes are supplied by municipal water supply systems that may be disabled by mega fatality initiators. Distress in these homes will begin within hours after the municipal water supply goes down and the residents will need to leave and seek water at refugee centers or other sources. Rural homes more typically rely on water wells with submersible electric pumps. If an electric power supply can be maintained for the pump, these homes should be OK indefinitely for water. Purification of available surface water is also an option but in nuclear war scenarios, radioactive contamination of surface water sources may be a problem.

Exhibit 20-3 Shelter Water Supply Ratings

Water supply capability	Water supply rating
Drinkable water storage for less than one week or a fresh water well without electric power backup	W0
Drinkable water storage for at least a week or a limited capacity purification system	W1
Drinkable water storage for at least 30 days or a robust purification system	W2
Fresh water well with electric power backup	W3

Sanitary waste disposal
A reliable sanitary waste disposal system is as essential for survival as a reliable water supply system and perhaps more so for urban residents. Like the water supply, virtually all urban and suburban homes are connected to a municipal sewage system. These systems may stop flowing and back up very quickly if electric power is lost, making many urban dwellings

uninhabitable. Rural homes, in contrast, typically rely on a passive septic system that requires no electric power to operate. Depending on the scenario and season, some suburban residents may be able to dig a latrine for temporary use.

Exhibit 20-4 Waste Disposal System Ratings

Waste disposal capability	Waste disposal rating
Municipal sewage system dependent on electric power	S0
Municipal sewage system capable of partial or temporary operation w/o electric power	S1
Latrine system	S2
Passive septic tank & drain field system	S3

Food supplies

Food supplies are an obvious necessity for any shelter. Presuming that the number of persons needing to be fed is known before the emergency occurs, the following rating system can be used to score the robustness of food supply preparations. At the top end of the rating scale is a shelter that has the capability produce food. If events do not unfold according to plan and the number of persons to be fed is larger than anticipated or the duration of need appears longer that planned for, then this assessment will need to be revised.

Exhibit 20-5 Shelter Food Supply Ratings

Food supply capability	Food supply rating
Food supplies are adequate to feed all occupants for at least one week	F0
Food supplies are adequate to feed all occupants for at least 30 days	F1
Food supplies are adequate to feed all occupants for at least one year	F2
Food supplies plus food production capabilities are adequate to feed all occupants indefinitely	F3

Electric grid independence

The need for electric power to operate essential survival shelter life support systems has already been discussed in other paragraphs. Here we will rate the robustness of the survival shelter's electric power system. In order to have a reliable electric power system, the needed electric load must be estimated accurately. Then, power sources capable of providing this need for a targeted duration can be selected and installed. If water is supplied from a well, a key electric load will be the well pump. This is typically a 240V, one horsepower + or − submersible pump/motor unit. Commercially available engine driven generators can easily generate sufficient power for the well pump and much more. Engines require gasoline, natural gas, or propane fuel, however, and the amount of fuel stored will set the duration that electric power can be generated without resupply. For long term sustainability renewable generating sources are needed. Solar panels and wind driven generators can be used as well as less expensive options like a bicycle driven generator that can provide both good exercise and needed power. Given the essential need for power, redundant and diverse generating sources are advisable to provide high reliability.

Exhibit 20-6 Electric Power System Ratings

Electric power system capability	Electric power system rating
Electric power is available only from batteries charged before the outage	P0
Electric power is available from an engine generator with a fuel supply good for at least one week	P1
Electric power is available from an engine generator with a fuel supply good for at least 30 days or renewable power from a single source	P2
Adequate electric power is available from diverse and redundant renewable sources	P3

Marauder protection

Even if you have prepared a shelter that meets or exceeds all the requirements discussed thus far, your survival may be very short lived if you neglect the need to protect it against marauders. If the emergency scenario that actually occurs is one where civil order is maintained outside the shelter, this may not be a key attribute. But for many mega fatality scenarios the maintenance of civil order cannot be assumed. Even if the interruption of civil order is only temporary, getting through that period unscathed is critical. In an urban setting particularly there may be bad actors that will exploit an emergency condition as an opportunity to raid and pillage others for no other reason than they might be able to get away with it.

Strategies for marauder protection can utilize camouflage or isolation to make the shelter hard for marauders to find, but most shelters will need to rely on some combination of fortifications and armaments for security. The following two rating scales can provide guidance on security preparations, but numerous exhaustive guides are available that provide much more detailed information. Remember, however, that marauder protection is not intended to be effective against the powerful weaponry that could be used during a military conflict scenario.

Exhibit 20-7 Shelter Defense Fortifications Ratings

Defense fortification provisions	Defense fortification rating
Normal housing structure w/o basement or reinforced shelter	D0
Normal housing structure with basement or reinforced shelter	D1
Reinforced structure w/o perimeter defenses & free fire zone	D2
Reinforced structure with perimeter defenses & free fire zone	D3

Exhibit 20-8 Shelter Armaments Ratings

Armament provisions	Armament rating
No armaments	A0
Handguns and low power firearms	A1
High power & automatic firearms	A2
High power & automatic firearms plus active perimeter defenses	A3

Risk Management Strategy Summary

I could continue to discuss more shelter attributes such as health and medical supplies and ventilation system capabilities, but I think that the eight rating tables already described in this chapter provide a good basis for defining survival shelter performance. Note that each rating table has four performance levels. So, we can define four general shelter performance levels by requiring that a shelter must meet the performance attributes of that level for each attribute to qualify for designation as a shelter of that level. In other words, a class 2 shelter must meet all attribute requirements to at least level 2 to earn that classification. Specific shelters can be scored by summing the points (0-3) awarded for their rating on each attribute and then dividing by eight. This score needs to be truncated, however, if a shelter has not scored the minimum rating needed for promotion to the next level. For example, if the sum of a shelter's ratings divided by eight comes to a score of 1.25 but it falls short of making level 1 on an attribute, then the classification score should be limited to (1-1/8) or 0.875. The next exhibit presents a simple worksheet that can be used to rate any specific shelter. An EXCEL version of the worksheet can also be downloaded from my website at jpkindinger.com.

Exhibit 20-9 Example Shelter Ranking

Shelter Attribute	Attribute Ranking (0 to 3)
Immediate hazard protection rating	1
Shelter exposure rating	1
Water supply rating	2
Waste disposal rating	2
Food supply rating	2
Electric power system rating	1
Defense fortification rating	1
Armament rating	0
Sum of rankings	10
Average score	1.25
Adjusted score	0.875

The real test of a survival shelter comes when we assess how it might perform under the high risk scenarios identified in the MFRA2 results. The final exhibit on the next page presents my assessment of this question for the four general shelter classes that are defined above. This is only a generic example. A specific shelter will need to be scored based on its own unique location, climate, and local hazard exposure. Once again, an EXCEL version of Exhibit 20-10 is available on my website that has blank columns and extra rows so it can be used in scoring your own personal risk management plan. A complete personal risk reduction plan should have at least one action (evacuation and/or shelter) that is not red (R) for each high risk hazard.

Exhibit 20-10 Generic Shelter Performance Rating

High Risk Hazards	Risk Reduction Strategies						
	Evacuation			Shelter			
General Hazards	R2	E0	E1	S0	S1	S2	S3
Moderate global cooling	Y	R	Y	R	Y	Y	G
Severe global cooling	Y	R	Y	R	Y	Y	G
Catastrophic global cooling	R	R	R	R	R	R	Y
Loss of electric power	Y	R	Y	R	Y	G	G
Pandemic	Y	Y	Y	R	R	Y	Y
Specific Local Hazards*							
Nuclear blast effects	G	R	R	R	R	R	Y
Conventional war	G	R	Y	R	R	R	R
Civil war or democide	G	Y	G	R	R	R	R
Earthquake	G	R	R	R	R	Y	G
Earthquake plus Tsunami	G	Y	G	R	Y	Y	G
Hurricane/cyclone	G	Y	G	Y	Y	G	G
Tornado	G	Y	G	R	Y	G	G
Flood	G	R	Y	R	Y	G	G
Fire	Y	Y	Y	Y	Y	G	G
High personal violence	G	R	Y	R	R	Y	Y
High health risk	G	R	Y	R	R	R	R

*may not be important at a specific location

Rating Key:
G significantly effective strategy for this hazard
Y marginally effective strategy for this hazard
R ineffective strategy for this hazard

Strategy Key:
R1- Proactive relocation away from hazard
E0- Evacuation on warning w/o advanced planning
E1- Evacuation on warning with advanced planning
S0- Refuge from hazard taken in a class 0 shelter
S1- Refuge from hazard taken in a class 1 shelter
S2- Refuge from hazard taken in a class 2 shelter
S3- Refuge from hazard taken in a class 3 shelter

Chapter 21 - The Endgame

Wow! I have covered a lot of different topics in *Survival Games* and it is now appropriate to summarize what I think are the most important findings.

First, we conducted a comprehensive search through the historical data on the frequency and consequences of human conflict. This revealed that the frequency of conflict has remained quite consistent for as long as we have good data and shows no sign of decreasing. The data for the consequences of conflict yielded a more complex story. As the technology of war making advanced through the nineteenth and twentieth centuries, the death toll mounted to peaks in WWI and WWII. Deaths from interstate war since WWII have been muted by the threat of nuclear holocaust, but the total conflict death toll was still driven to new highs by the democide of powerless populations by their own autocratic governments.

Next, we examined the potential consequences of nuclear war, should it ever occur. Objective estimates indicate that an unlimited exchange of strategic nuclear weapons between the USA and Russia targeted on cities could kill a high percentage of the populations of both nations. Beyond mutually assured destruction of the combatants, an exchange of as few as 100 weapons between any of the nuclear weapons states could initiate a global cooling event that would kill massive numbers worldwide and even threaten human extinction. With conditional consequences this high, the likelihood of nuclear war obviously becomes a key element needed to understand mega fatality risk.

To make an estimate of nuclear war likelihood I reached into the risk assessment tool kit and constructed a master logic diagram (MLD) that described the possible pathways that could result in the detonation of nuclear weapons. I then systematically walked through all the MLD paths to make estimates of their frequency. The most difficult of these paths was the intentional use of these weapons. To provide perspective on this possibility, I developed a two-step qualitative ranking system. In the first step, I identified the most contentious conflict points between the nuclear weapons states and ranked their current potential for conflict initiation and escalation to nuclear conflict. In the second step of the qualitative analysis, I assessed the capability, or incapability, of each nuclear weapons state to sustain the current geopolitical equilibrium in which nuclear war has been avoided. This assessment identified Korea as the most likely conflict theater for nuclear war and Syria/Iraq as the highest total risk conflict because of its potential for escalating into a USA-Russia nuclear war. The second step of the analysis also identified the USA as the nuclear weapons state with the greatest potential for causing instability in the fragile game of nuclear brinksmanship.

I then incorporated these findings on nuclear war risk into a comprehensive update of the mega fatality risk assessment (MFRA) first presented in *Risk Management Revisited* (*RMR*). The results of this update showed nuclear war to be the dominant contributor to mega fatality risk with decreased but still significant contributions from conventional war and pandemics. The MFRA2 update also confirmed the importance of long term loss of electric power scenarios as the second biggest source of mega fatality risk.

Building on the updated results for mega fatality risk, I then expanded the risk picture to also include all normal individual fatality risks and presented a framework that allows both normal individual risk and mega fatality risk to be viewed in proper perspective. With this complete view of fatality risk, an objective and risk informed basis for identifying possible risk reduction strategies is possible. The book then concludes with some suggested tools that can be used by individuals and families to help win the *Survival Games*.

I would be remiss, however, if I do not conclude *Survival Games* with a note of hope for the future. As my red team readers quickly pointed out, I have painted a pretty bleak picture of the future and perhaps give too little credit to the re-inventive power of the American people. With this in mind let me point out that although I have characterized nuclear war as clear and present danger, it is by no means inevitable.

Still, the challenges I highlight that face the American people and their government need to be faced head-on soon or events will spin out of control. Can the expansion of the welfare state that drives mandatory spending be brought under control? Has the debt plus promised future benefits already passed the point of no return for survival of the U.S. Government as presently constituted? What would a world order without U.S. dominance look like? And, how can an orderly transition from the current world order to that new future be engineered? These are questions for which I have no answers. Maybe for the next project.....

Appendix A – American Debticide

> **Debticide** – The condition where a government is unable to defend its vital interests due to chronic fiscal irresponsibility and the accumulation of unsustainable debt.

The primary finding of this book is that the dominant contributor to mega fatality risk is a nuclear war triggered by the debt forced weakening of the American deterrence shield that has been in place over the western democracies since World War II. This uncontrolled weakening of the American deterrence shield is brought about by the financial degeneration of the United States government which in turn forces a redefinition of American vital interests and the creation of a new world order where the United States is not dominant. The task of forming this new world order is a diplomatic, economic, and military challenge without precedence and one that is fraught with the risk of war.

Although many before me have pointed to the dangers of the U. S. Government's financial irresponsibility, I believe no one has made the connection to human mega fatality risk as explicitly as I have. As a result, I felt the need to provide more than just references to other work as a justification for these findings. So, I elected to apply my own limited abilities to an examination of the financial condition of the United States Government. Here it goes.

The Task

The objective of this analysis is to project the ability, or not, of the U. S. government to maintain defense expenditures sufficient to sustain the deterrence shield over the western democracies that has been in place since World War II. Based purely on recent historical data, I required a continuing spending stream equal to 4% of U. S. GDP to satisfy this strategic interest. Significantly larger defense expenditures were sustained during the Cold War years and many may argue that

4% is insufficient. Others may assert that the U. S. could get by with less defense spending if it adopted more "progressive" policies toward other nations.

The Model and Success Criteria

The analysis of U. S. defense spending capability was performed with a spreadsheet model built upon revenue and spending category definitions and historical unified budget data provided by the Congressional Budget Office (CBO). The U. S. capacity for discretionary spending was calculated by subtracting projected mandatory spending and interest expense from an available budget pegged at actual tax revenues plus an allowed annual deficit set at 3.5% of GDP for base case calculations. Available discretionary funds are then assumed to be split evenly between defense needs and the needs of all other government activities. If the amount available for defense spending is less than the defense needs, then the difference is recorded as a *defense deficit*. I further stipulate that if the cumulative defense deficit across multiple years accumulates to more than one trillion dollars, then the deterrence mission is no longer credible and the risk of nuclear war increases dramatically. The term I have coined to describe this condition is *debticide*. This is of course an arbitrary definition. Nothing dramatic will automatically happen when the defense deficit crosses one trillion dollars. The symptoms of a coming debticide should include:

- The accumulation of excessive government debt levels
- The use of deceptive financial practices to obscure debt levels or artificially suppress interest rates
- Increasing social unrest and political vitriol in response to unmet social welfare promises and a growing sense of government impotence
- Diminishing conventional military capability as measured by the numbers of uniformed personnel, ships, planes, etc.
- Reduced readiness levels for operational military forces
- Increased belligerence in the behavior of the autocratic nuclear weapons states toward the U.S. and its allies

- Inconsistency in the response of the U.S. and its allies to these belligerent acts by the autocratic nuclear weapons states
- Open expressions of mistrust among the U.S. and its allies

The scenario I have assumed for this analysis is a "slow debticide" where the symptoms of debticide build over time to a critical confrontation that may occur before or after my one trillion dollar milestone. If debticide follows the pattern of other American crises, political myopia will prevent meaningful change until the occurrence of the critical confrontation. But this time American leaders will find themselves faced with a no-win choice of nuclear weapons use or capitulation to an adversary. *Survival Games* assesses the likelihood of nuclear war resulting from such a crisis and the immediate consequences of the conflict.

As I described in Chapter 12, the critical confrontation that would mark the culmination of debticide could also be deliberately provoked by economic warfare. Since the U.S. government is already vulnerable to such an attack, this "fast debticide" could happen at any time. But the choice of waging economic or military war is merely a tactical one, the principle concept being that a financially weakened USA invites increased aggression.

Mandatory Spending

A critical element in the defense debt analysis is the estimation of mandatory spending. Per the CBO, the following items compose the mandatory spending accounts of the U. S. government.

- Social Security
- Medicare
- Medicaid
- Income Security
- Federal Civilian and Military Retirement
- Veterans' Programs

- Other Smaller Programs

Actual outlays for these accounts for the last 15 years are as follows.

Mandatory Spending Data

Year	Mandatory Spending	Mandatory % Growth
2000	951	
2001	1,008	5.91%
2002	1,106	9.76%
2003	1,182	6.92%
2004	1,238	4.65%
2005	1,319	6.62%
2006	1,412	7.00%
2007	1,450	2.70%
2008	1,595	9.99%
2009	2,093	31.25%
2010	1,914	-8.58%
2011	2,026	5.87%
2012	2,030	0.22%
2013	2,032	0.06%
2014	2,098	3.29%
2015	2,297	9.44%
2016	2,429	5.78%
average		6.31%

Debt and the Deficit

Much public attention is given to the amounts of the annual deficit and the "national debt". It turns out that identifying what these sums are isn't so simple. The national debt is actually composed of the following three components.

	2016 B$
Debt Held by Public	14,168
Debt Held by Gov	5,369
Agency Debt	8,377
Total Fed Gov Debt	27,914

The debt held by the public is all debt held by individuals and institutions outside of the United States Government. The debt held by the government belongs to statutory trust funds like Social Security and Medicare. The debt held by the public and the government are commonly added together and labeled as the total "on budget" debt. This amount was $19.537 trillion as of the end of FY 2016. Agency debt is issued by chartered agencies like Federal National Mortgage Association (FNMA) and Federal Home Loan Mortgage Corporation (FHLMC). Because this debt is supposed to be repaid by third parties, like home owners, it is "off budget" and not counted as part of the official national debt. As we saw in 2008, however, "off budget" can suddenly become on budget if the debt goes sour.

Interest is technically paid on all the on budget debt, but since the interest on the government held debt just moves from one hand to the other, it is netted out in the budget data. Because of this, our model accounts only for interest paid on the publically held debt. Accounting for the trust funds also causes another interesting quirk in the data. Most rational people, I think, would expect the national debt to rise each year by the amount of the deficit for that year. Or algebraically:

Year end debt = Year beginning debt + the deficit

However, this math does not work. The debt is rising much faster than this equation indicates. This happens because the statutory trust funds are spending more than they bring in and are cashing in their treasury bonds to pay benefits. Since the Treasury spent the money received from these bond sales long ago, it has no reserves and must borrow new money to pay the trust funds. Thus, each year they must borrow much more money than the deficit indicates. Who knew? This accounting artifact will disappear in the near future, however, because the trust funds are shrinking like a snow pile in June and are projected to be depleted between 2022 and 2034.

Analysis Results

The primary metric calculated by the defense deficit model is the year in which the cumulative defense deficit is indicated to cross the one trillion dollar threshold. The actual analysis spreadsheet is too large to include in this book. A PDF copy is available for the curious on my website at **jpkindinger.com**. The following table summarizes the results of several different cases I have run with the model to explore sensitivity in the results.

Defense Deficit Analysis Results Summary

Case		Debticide Date
#	Short Description	
1	Base case, stay the current course	2022
2	Higher GDP growth	2025
3	Much higher tax revenue	2034
4	Long term low interest rates	2024
5	High inflation	2021
6	Recession shock in 2020	2021
7	Lower mandatory spending growth	2025
8	Much lower mandatory spending growth	never
9	Balanced budget & mandatory spending freeze beginning in 2020	2021

Only in Case #8 where the growth of mandatory spending is reduced below the growth of GDP is debticide avoided. Case #9 presents an interesting result where the defense deficit rapidly rises above the one trillion dollar milestone and peaks at about 3.3 trillion in 2028 but then reverses and shrinks below the debticide level by 2044. Additional information about each of these sensitivity cases is presented in the exhibits that follow in the balance of this appendix.

In summary, the analysis results indicate that a severe reduction in mandatory spending needs to be in enacted now! The predicted debticide dates for all cases with uncontrolled mandatory spending are almost upon us. I would like to be optimistic and believe that our political leaders see this calamity coming and will take the actions necessary to avoid debticide, but I have no evidence to offer in support of that hope.

Defense Deficit Analysis

Case 1	Base Case
Case Description - Base case with revenue and spending growth projected at an average of the rates experienced over the last 15 years. The interest rate paid on the debt rises to the long term average for the 10 year treasury bond.	

Year of projected debticide [**2022**]

Rate Data

3.78%	Current dollar GDP growth rate
6.31%	Mandatory spending growth rate
4.00%	Defense spending needs (% of GDP)
20.00%	Politically acceptable tax revenue rate (% of GDP)
3.50%	Sustainable deficit (% of GDP)
10.00%	Maximum one year deficit (% of GDP)
4.54%	Average long term interest rate on debt

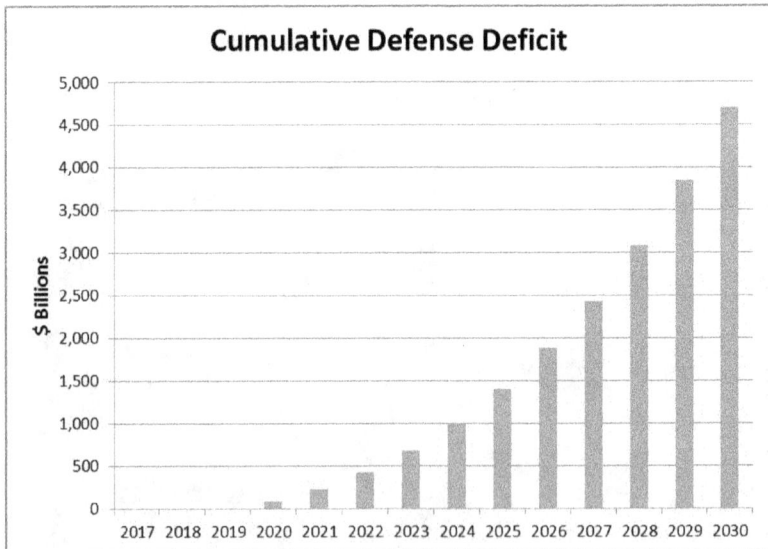

Cumulative Defense Deficit

Defense Deficit Analysis

Case 2	**Consistently High GDP growth**

Case Description - All data is the same as the base case except nominal GDP growth is increased to 5.5 % per year

Year of projected debticide [**2025**]

Rate Data

5.50%	Current dollar GDP growth rate
6.31%	Mandatory spending growth rate
4.00%	Defense spending needs (% of GDP)
20.00%	Politically acceptable tax revenue rate (% of GDP)
3.50%	Sustainable deficit (% of GDP)
10.00%	Maximum one year deficit (% of GDP)
4.54%	Average long term interest rate on debt

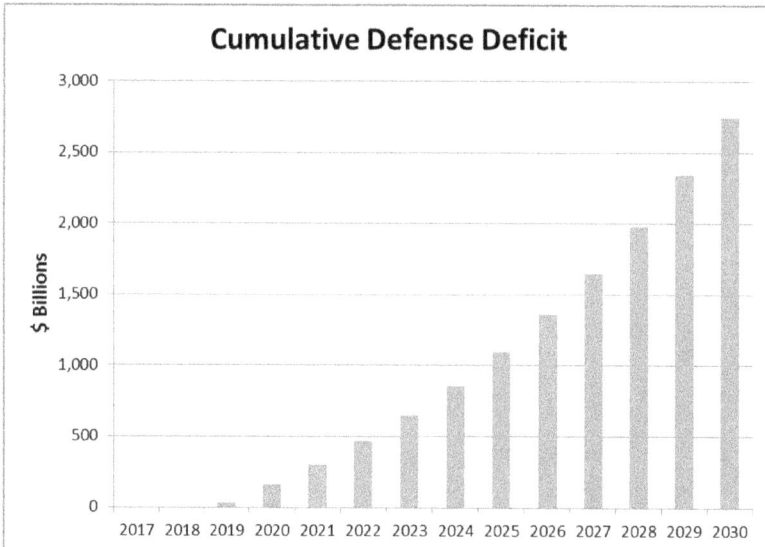

Cumulative Defense Deficit

Defense Deficit Analysis

Case 3	**Much higher tax revenue**

Case Description - All data is the same as the base case except tax revenues are increased to 25% of GDP. Many would expect that GDP growth would be negatively impacted by higher taxes, but no allowance for that was included in this case.

Year of projected debticide | **2034**

Rate Data

3.78%	Current dollar GDP growth rate
6.31%	Mandatory spending growth rate
4.00%	Defense spending needs (% of GDP)
25.00%	Politically acceptable tax revenue rate (% of GDP)
3.50%	Sustainable deficit (% of GDP)
10.00%	Maximum one year deficit (% of GDP)
4.54%	Average long term interest rate on debt

Cumulative Defense Deficit

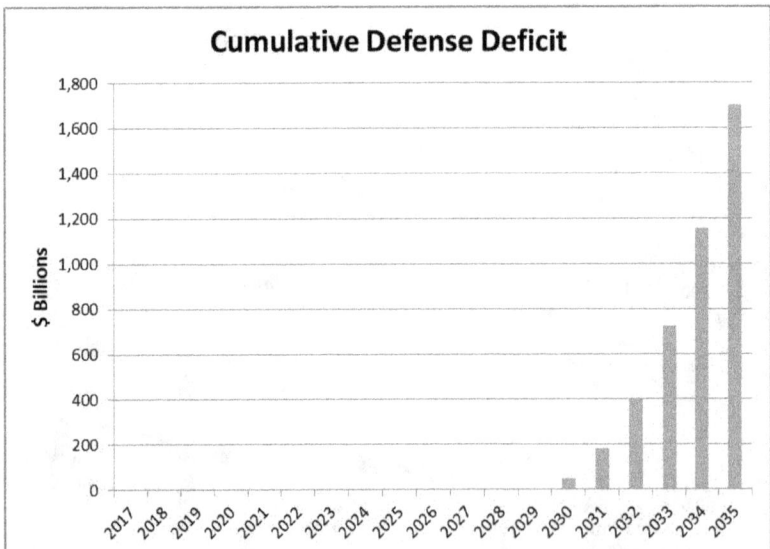

Defense Deficit Analysis

Case 4	Long term low interest rates
Case Description - All data is the same as the base case except interest paid on the debt is capped at 3.0 % per year	
Year of projected debticide	**2024**

Rate Data

3.78%	Current dollar GDP growth rate
6.31%	Mandatory spending growth rate
4.00%	Defense spending needs (% of GDP)
20.00%	Politically acceptable tax revenue rate (% of GDP)
3.50%	Sustainable deficit (% of GDP)
10.00%	Maximum one year deficit (% of GDP)
3.00%	Average long term interest rate on debt

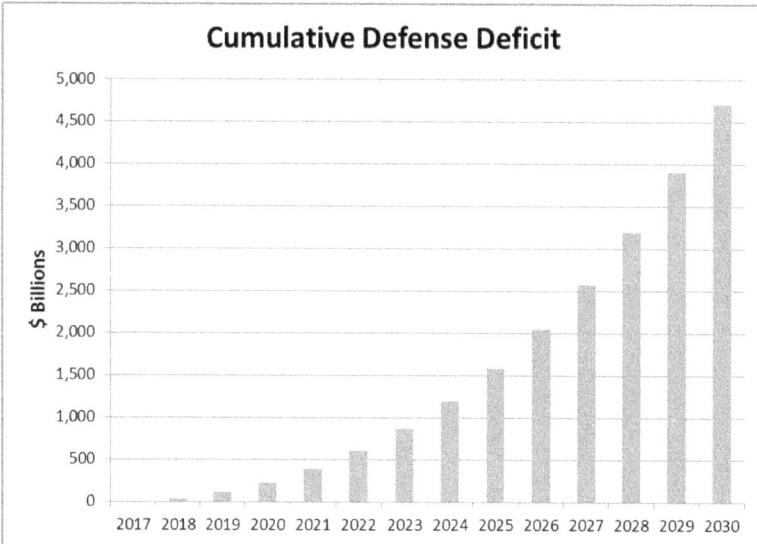

Cumulative Defense Deficit

Defense Deficit Analysis

Case 5	High inflation

Case Description - All data is the same as the base case except rates for GDP growth, mandatory spending growth, and interest are all doubled to reflect high inflation.

Year of projected debticide | **2021**

Rate Data

Rate	Description
7.56%	Current dollar GDP growth rate
12.62%	Mandatory spending growth rate
4.00%	Defense spending needs (% of GDP)
20.00%	Politically acceptable tax revenue rate (% of GDP)
3.50%	Sustainable deficit (% of GDP)
10.00%	Maximum one year deficit (% of GDP)
9.08%	Average long term interest rate on debt

Cumulative Defense Deficit

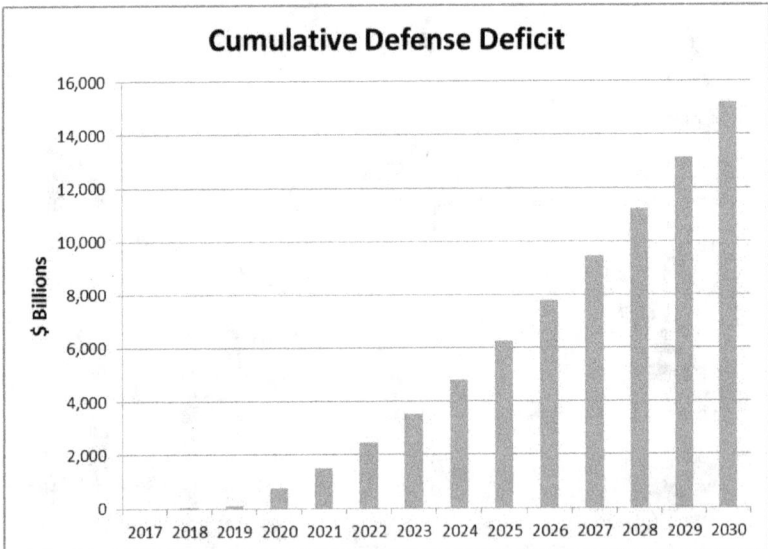

Defense Deficit Analysis

Case 6	**Recession shock in 2020**

Case Description - All data is the same as the base case except a recession in 2020 causes GDP to decrease 2% and mandatory spending to increase by 15%. Nominal growth rates are assumed to resume in 2021 and beyond.

Year of projected debticide | **2021**

Rate Data

3.78%	Current dollar GDP growth rate
6.31%	Mandatory spending growth rate
4.00%	Defense spending needs (% of GDP)
20.00%	Politically acceptable tax revenue rate (% of GDP)
3.50%	Sustainable deficit (% of GDP)
10.00%	Maximum one year deficit (% of GDP)
4.54%	Average long term interest rate on debt

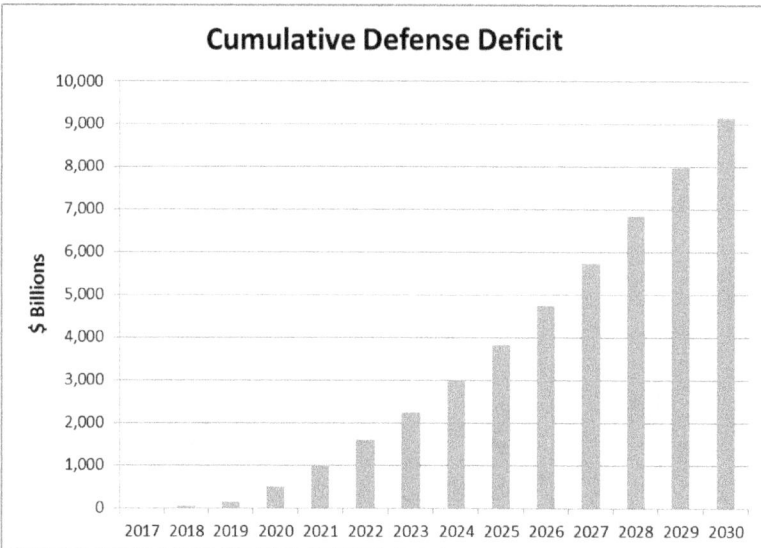

Cumulative Defense Deficit

Defense Deficit Analysis

Case 7	Lower mandatory spending growth
Case Description - All data is the same as the base case except the growth rate of mandatory spending is reduced to 4% per year.	

Year of projected debticide | 2025 |

Rate Data

3.78%	Current dollar GDP growth rate
4.00%	Mandatory spending growth rate
4.00%	Defense spending needs (% of GDP)
20.00%	Politically acceptable tax revenue rate (% of GDP)
3.50%	Sustainable deficit (% of GDP)
10.00%	Maximum one year deficit (% of GDP)
4.54%	Average long term interest rate on debt

Cumulative Defense Deficit

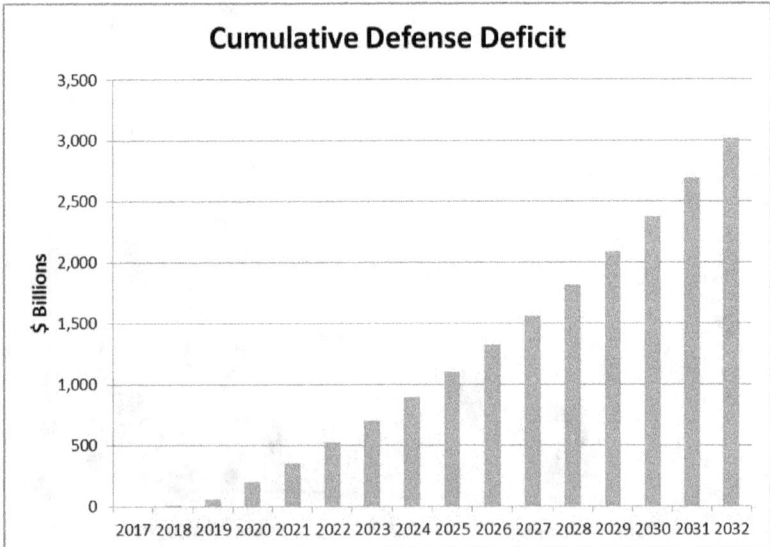

Defense Deficit Analysis

Case 8	Much lower mandatory spending growth

Case Description - All data is the same as the base case except the growth rate of mandatory spending is reduced to 3% per year.

Year of projected debticide **never**

Rate Data

3.78%	Current dollar GDP growth rate
3.00%	Mandatory spending growth rate
4.00%	Defense spending needs (% of GDP)
20.00%	Politically acceptable tax revenue rate (% of GDP)
3.50%	Sustainable deficit (% of GDP)
10.00%	Maximum one year deficit (% of GDP)
4.54%	Average long term interest rate on debt

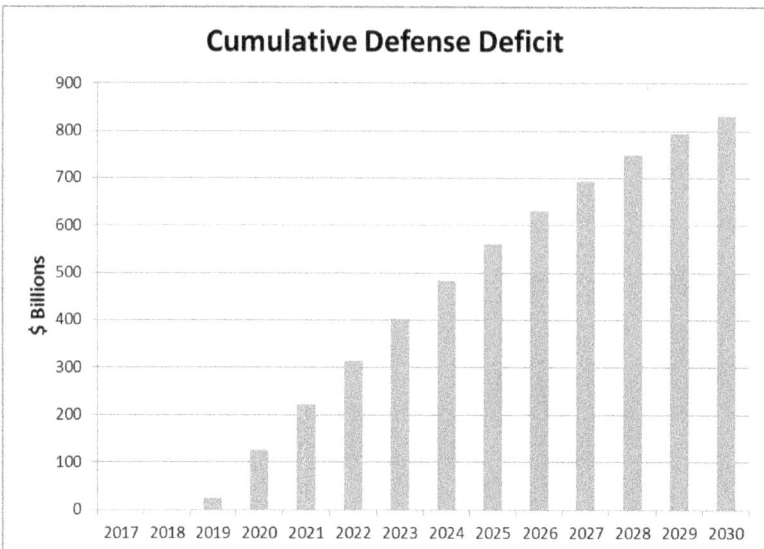

Cumulative Defense Deficit

Defense Deficit Analysis

Case 9	Budget balanced & mandatory spending frozen

Case Description - All data is the same as the base case except budget outlays are limited not to exceed tax revenues and mandatory spending is frozen (zero growth) starting in 2020.

Year of projected debticide **never**

Rate Data

3.78%	Current dollar GDP growth rate
0.00%	Mandatory spending growth rate
4.00%	Defense spending needs (% of GDP)
20.00%	Politically acceptable tax revenue rate (% of GDP)
0.00%	Sustainable deficit (% of GDP)
10.00%	Maximum one year deficit (% of GDP)
4.54%	Average long term interest rate on debt

Cumulative Defense Deficit

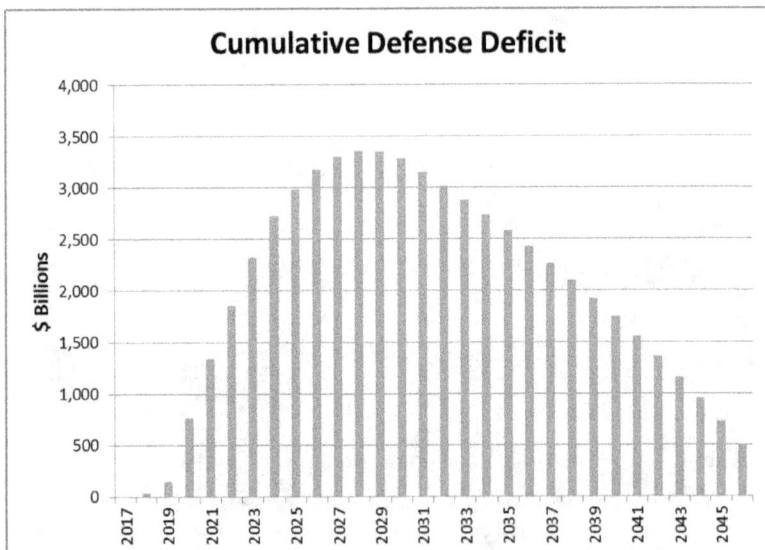

194

Appendix A References:

A-1. *The Budget and Economic Outlook: 2017 to 2027,* Congressional Budget Office, January 2017.

A-2. The 2017 Annual Report of the Board of Trustees of the Federal Old-Age and Survivors Insurance and Federal Disability Insurance Trust Funds, 7/13/2017.

A-3. The Debt to the Penny and Who Holds It, US treasurydirect.gov

A-4. www.usgovernmentdebt.us, Christopher Chantrill

A-5. Financial and Sovereign Debt Crises: Some Lessons Learned and Those Forgotten, Carmen M. Reinhart and Kenneth S. Rogoff, *International Monetary Fund,* WP/13/266, December 2013

A-6. Financial Repression Redux, Carmen M. Reinhart, Jacob F. Kirkegaard, and M. Belen Sbrancia, *Finance & Development,* June 2011

A-7. Obstacle to Deficit Cutting: A Nation on Entitlements, Sara Murray, *The Wall Street Journal,* 9/15/2010

A-8. The Magnitude of the Mess We're In, George P. Schultz, et al, *The Wall Street Journal,* 9/17/2012

A-9. Why $16 Trillion Only Hints at the True U.S. Debt, Chris Cox and Bill Archer, , *The Wall Street Journal,* 11/28/2012

A-10. *Is the U.S. Current Account Deficit Sustainable?* , Sebastian Edwards, NBER Working Paper No. 11541, August 2005

A-11. *Debt and (not much) Deleveraging,* McKinsey Global Institute, February 2015.

A-12. *Solving the Triffin Dilemma,* John D. Mueller, Kemp Forum on Exchange Rates and the Dollar, 4/20/2017

Appendix B – MFRA2 Excel/Crystal Ball Model

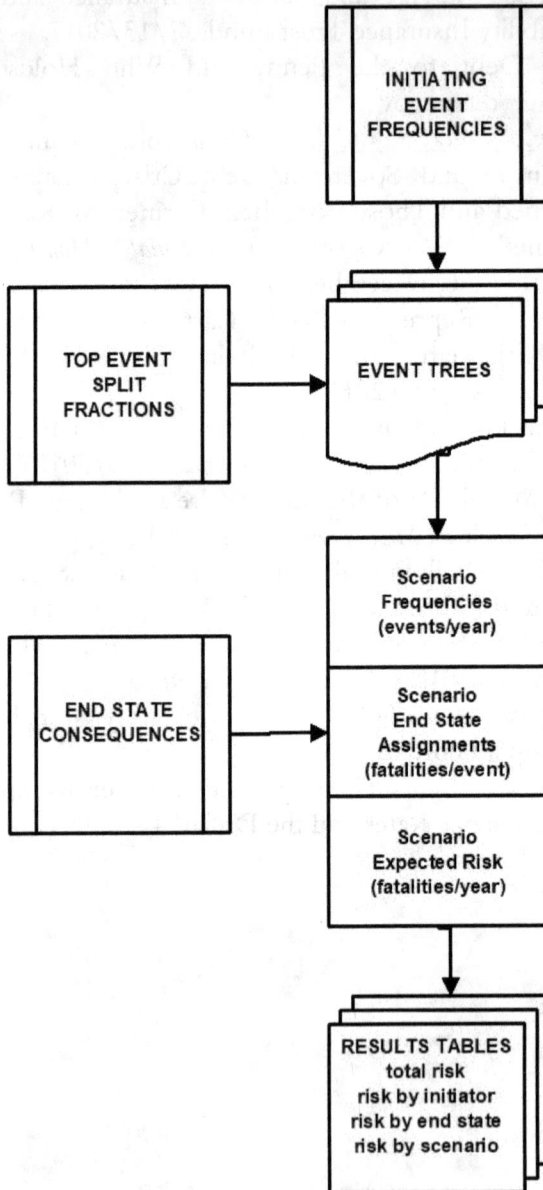

```
                                    ┌──┬──────────────┬──┐
                                    │  │ INITIATING   │  │
                                    │  │ EVENT        │  │
                                    │  │ FREQUENCIES  │  │
                                    └──┴──────────────┴──┘
                                            │
                                            ▼
┌──┬──────────────┬──┐        ┌──┬──────────────┬──┐
│  │ TOP EVENT    │  │        │  │              │  │
│  │ SPLIT        │  │ ─────▶ │  │ EVENT TREES  │  │
│  │ FRACTIONS    │  │        │  │              │  │
└──┴──────────────┴──┘        └──┴──────────────┴──┘
                                            │
                                            ▼
                              ┌─────────────────────────┐
                              │     Scenario            │
                              │     Frequencies         │
                              │     (events/year)       │
                              ├─────────────────────────┤
┌──┬──────────────┬──┐        │     Scenario            │
│  │ END STATE    │  │ ─────▶ │     End State           │
│  │ CONSEQUENCES │  │        │     Assignments         │
│  │              │  │        │     (fatalities/event)  │
└──┴──────────────┴──┘        ├─────────────────────────┤
                              │     Scenario            │
                              │     Expected Risk       │
                              │     (fatalities/year)   │
                              └─────────────────────────┘
                                            │
                                            ▼
                              ┌─────────────────────────┐
                              │  RESULTS TABLES         │
                              │  total risk             │
                              │  risk by initiator      │
                              │  risk by end state      │
                              │  risk by scenario       │
                              └─────────────────────────┘
```

Initiator		Calculated	Form	Distribution						Source
Code	Description	Mean		%tile	Value	%tile	Value	%tile	Value	References
Cosmic Events										
KI10m	Kinetic impact of 10 m object	1.3E-01	T	0	0.01	50	0.1	100	0.25	Reference #2
KI100m	Kinetic impact of 100 m object	3.2E-04	LN	mean	1.92E-04	RF	5	95	1.00E-03	Reference #2
KI1km	Kinetic impact of 1 km object	5.7E-06	LN	mean	2.27E-06	RF	5	95	1.14E-05	Reference #2
KI10km	Kinetic impact of 10 km object	4.0E-08	LN	mean	1.52E-08	RF	10	95	1.50E-07	Reference #2
SolStrm	Solar storm	3.7E-03	LN	50	3.00E-03	95	9.0E-03			Reference #22
Natural Terrestrial Events										
SuperV7	VEI category 7 volcanic eruption	2.7E-05	LN	mean	2.5E-05	RF	2	95	5.00E-05	Reference #10
SuperV8	VEI category 8 volcanic eruption	8.2E-06	LN	mean	7.5E-06	RF	2	95	1.50E-05	Reference #10
Mquake	Mega Earthquake	9.3E-01	LN	mean	7.9E-01	95	1.6E+00			Reference #13
Mflood	Other flood event	3.5E-03	LN	mean	3.0E-03	95	6.0E-03			Reference #14
Pandemic Events										
NatEpid	High severity natural epidemic	4.4E-02	LN	mean	0.04	RF	2	95	0.08	Chapter 14
bioaccident	Accidental release of known disease	4.9E-02	T	0	0.021	50	0.042	100	0.084	Chapter 14
bioattack	Release of weaponized pathogen	6.8E-04	LN	mean	6.25E-04	RF	2	95	1.25E-03	Chapter 13
biolabsab	Biological laboratory sabotage	6.1E-03	LN	mean	5.63E-03	RF	2	95	1.13E-02	Chapter 13
Terrorist Attacks										
epsabotage	Electric power system sabotage	1.4E-02	LN	mean	1.25E-02	RF	2	95	2.50E-02	Chapter 13
nucdet	Nuclear terrorist attack	6.8E-03	LN	mean	6.25E-03	RF	2	95	1.25E-02	Chapter 13
Human Conflict										
armcon	Conventional armed conflict	3.08	T	0	1	50	3.25	100	5	Chapter 2
lofw	Nuclear first strike on false warning	5.8E-04	T	0	2.50E-04	50	5.0E-04	100	1.00E-03	Chapter 9
India1	Nuclear first strike by India1	3.0E-05	T	0	1.00E-05	50	3.0E-05	100	5.00E-05	Chapter 11 & 12
Pakistan	Nuclear first strike by Pakistan	3.0E-04	T	0	1.00E-04	50	3.0E-04	100	5.00E-04	Chapter 11 & 12
India2	Nuclear first strike by India2	3.0E-05	T	0	1.00E-05	50	3.0E-05	100	5.00E-05	Chapter 11 & 12
China1	Nuclear first strike by China1	3.0E-05	T	0	1.00E-05	50	3.0E-05	100	5.00E-05	Chapter 11 & 12
N Korea	Nuclear first strike by N Korea	3.0E-03	T	0	1.00E-03	50	3.0E-03	100	5.00E-03	Chapter 11 & 12
USA1	Nuclear first strike by USA1	3.0E-03	T	0	1.00E-03	50	3.0E-03	100	5.00E-03	Chapter 11 & 12
China2	Nuclear first strike by China2	3.0E-05	T	0	1.00E-05	50	3.0E-05	100	5.00E-05	Chapter 11 & 12
USA2	Nuclear first strike by USA2	3.0E-04	T	0	1.00E-04	50	3.0E-04	100	5.00E-04	Chapter 11 & 12
Russia1	Nuclear first strike by Russia1	3.0E-04	T	0	1.00E-04	50	3.0E-04	100	5.00E-04	Chapter 11 & 12
NATO/USA3	Nuclear first strike by USA3	3.0E-04	T	0	1.00E-04	50	3.0E-04	100	5.00E-04	Chapter 11 & 12
Russia2	Nuclear first strike by Russia2	3.0E-05	T	0	1.00E-05	50	3.0E-05	100	5.00E-05	Chapter 11 & 12
NATO/USA4	Nuclear first strike by USA4	3.0E-04	T	0	1.00E-04	50	3.0E-04	100	5.00E-04	Chapter 11 & 12
Russia3	Nuclear first strike by Russia3	3.0E-04	T	0	1.00E-04	50	3.0E-04	100	5.00E-04	Chapter 11 & 12
NATO/USA5	Nuclear first strike by USA5	3.0E-03	T	0	1.00E-03	50	3.0E-03	100	5.00E-03	Chapter 11 & 12
Iran	Nuclear first strike by Iran	3.0E-05	T	0	1.00E-05	50	3.0E-05	100	5.00E-05	Chapter 11 & 12
Israel	Nuclear first strike by Israel	3.0E-05	T	0	1.00E-05	50	3.0E-05	100	5.00E-05	Chapter 11 & 12
China3	Nuclear first strike by China3	3.0E-04	T	0	1.00E-04	50	3.0E-04	100	5.00E-04	Chapter 11 & 12
USA6	Nuclear first strike by USA6	3.0E-03	T	0	1.00E-03	50	3.0E-03	100	5.00E-03	Chapter 11 & 12

Split Fraction Data

Initiator		calculated	Distribution							Source References
Code	Description	Mean	Form	%tile	Value	%tile	Value	%tile	Value	
				0	0.01	50	0.02	100	0.05	
HPZ	Probability of impact in high population zone	0.03	T	0	0.01	50	0.02	100	0.05	550 cities w > 1M people, a hit within a 50 mi radius of each gives a target of 4.3 mil sq mi or ~ 2%
LAND	Probability of impact on land	0.29								
SF	Bio lab security measures fail to prevent release	0.50	T	0	0.05	50	0.5	100	0.95	JPK estimate
CFH	Containment failure for high severity pathogen	0.04	T	0	0.005	50	0.01	100	0.1	JPK estimate
CFX	Containment failure following bio lab attack	0.19	T	0	0.01	50	0.05	100	0.5	JPK estimate
CFXX	Containment failure following bio attack	0.38	T	0	0.05	50	0.1	100	1	
SLSP	Failure of SLS systems during pandemic	0.50	T	0	0.25	50	0.5	100	0.75	JPK estimate
SLSEP	Failure of SLS systems during extended EP outage	0.50	T	0	0.25	50	0.5	100	0.75	JPK estimate
EPCW	EP sabotage results in continent wide outage	0.38	T	0	0.05	50	0.1	100	1	JPK estimate
NWHY	Terrorist nuclear weapon is high yield	0.05	T	0	0.01	50	0.05	100	0.1	JPK estimate
CW	Probability that a mega conflict is a civil war	0.70								14/20
MEGAC	Probability of mega fatality conflict	3.18E-02								20/630
DCW	Probability of democide in a civil war	0.42								6/14
GC1	Probability of global cooling with <100 weapons	0.00								
GC2	Probability of global cooling with <250 weapons	0.57	T	0	0.000	50	0.800	100	0.900	

End State Data

Code	Description	Mean Fatalities	Form	%ile	Value	%ile	Value	%ile	Value	Basis
	End State Data					Distribution (fatalities)				
nomega	Not a mega fatality scenario									
PF10m	10 m asteroid impact on high population zone	1.2E+06	LN	mean	5.0E+05	95	4.5E+06	RF	9.0	Chapter 14 analysis
pff100m	100 m impact asteroid impact	1.6E+07	LN	mean	1.5E+07	95	3.0E+07	RF	2.0	Reference 4
chaos1	10 million affected by SLS failure	2.5E+06	LN	mean	2.0E+06	95	6.0E+06	RF	3.0	Chapters 13 & 15
chaos2	100 million affected by SLS failure	2.5E+07	LN	mean	2.0E+07	95	6.0E+07	RF	3.0	Chapters 13 & 15
chaos3	500 million affected by SLS failure	1.2E+08	LN	mean	1.0E+08	95	3.0E+08	RF	3.0	Chapters 13 & 15
chaos4	2 billion affected by SLS failure	5.0E+08	LN	mean	4.0E+08	95	1.2E+09	RF	3.0	Chapters 13 & 15
chaos5	7 billion affected by SLS failure	1.8E+09	LN	mean	1.4E+09	95	4.2E+09	RF	3.0	Chapters 13 & 15
equake	direct fatalities + local chaos	2.6E+06	T	0	5.0E+03	50	3.0E+05	100	7.5E+06	MFRA
flood	direct fatalities + local chaos	5.6E+06	T	0	5.0E+05	50	1.3E+06	100	1.5E+07	MFRA
pand4	high severity w effective containment	9.7E+06	LN	mean	6.0E+06	95	3.0E+07	RF	5.0	Chapter 15
pand5	high severity w/o effective containment	6.4E+07	LN	mean	4.0E+07	95	2.0E+08	RF	5.0	Chapter 15
pand5p	high severity w/o effective containment + global SLS breakdown	1.2E+08	LN	mean	8.0E+07	95	4.0E+08	RF	5.0	Chapter 15
nucattack	Low yield nuclear detonation	3.9E+05	LN	mean	1.3E+05	95	1.5E+06	RF	11.5	Chapter 6 analysis
nucattackp	High yield nuclear detonation	6.6E+05	LN	mean	2.5E+05	95	2.5E+06	RF	10.0	Chapter 6 analysis
cwdths	Mega fatality civil war	1.1E+06	LN	mean	1.0E+06	95	2.0E+06	RF	2.0	Chapter 2 data
demodths	Mega fatality civil war + democide	1.9E+07	T	0	1.0E+06	50	5.0E+06	100	5.0E+07	Chapter 2 data
iswardths	Mega fatality interstate war	1.7E+07	LN	mean	1.1E+07	95	5.0E+07	RF	4.5	Chapter 2 data
twhd100	Nuc war w <100 tactical warheads used	5.8E+06	T	0	2.5E+06	50	5.0E+06	100	1.0E+07	Chapter 6 analysis
twhd100+	Nuc war w <100 tactical warheads + EMP	1.5E+08	T	0	6.3E+07	50	1.3E+08	100	2.5E+08	Chapter 6 analysis
twhd200	Nuc war w <200 tactical warheads	1.2E+07	T	0	5.0E+06	50	1.0E+07	100	2.0E+07	Chapter 6 analysis
swhd10	Nuc war w <10 strategic warheads used	5.6E+06	T	0	2.6E+06	50	5.5E+06	100	1.1E+07	Chapter 6 analysis
swhd50	Nuc war w <50 strategic warheads used	3.3E+07	T	0	1.5E+07	50	2.8E+07	100	5.5E+07	Chapter 6 analysis
swhd50p	Nuc war w <50 strategic warheads + EMP	5.8E+07	T	0	2.5E+07	50	5.0E+07	100	1.0E+08	Chapter 6 analysis
swhd120	Nuc war w 100 to 250 strategic warheads used	7.6E+07	T	0	3.3E+07	50	6.6E+07	100	1.3E+08	Chapter 6 analysis
gcm	Global cooling moderate & nuc war w 250 to 500 strategic warheads used	8.3E+08	T	0	3.6E+08	50	7.2E+08	100	1.4E+09	Chapter 6 analysis
gcs	Global cooling severe & nuc war w 1000 to 1750 strategic warheads used	3.2E+09	T	0	7.2E+08	50	3.6E+09	100	5.4E+09	Chapter 6 analysis
gcc	Global cooling catastrophic & nuc war w >3000 strategic warheads used	5.8E+09	T	0	3.6E+09	50	6.8E+09	100	7.2E+09	Chapter 6 analysis

Kinetic Impacts Event Trees

Initiator	Impact in low population area?	#	Frequency (events/yr)	End State	Risk (PF/yr)	Comments
KI10m	Yes	1	1.2E-01	nomega		
1.3E-01	HPZ	2	3.4E-03	PF10m	4.1E+03	impact in high pop area

Initiator	Water Impact?	#	Frequency (events/yr)	End State	Risk (PF/yr)	Comments
KI100m	Yes	1	2.3E-04	pf100m	3.7E+03	water impact
3.2E-04	LAND	2	9.2E-05	gcm	7.6E+04	land impact

Initiator	Water Impact?	#	Frequency (events/yr)	End State	Risk (PF/yr)	Comments
KI1km	Yes	1	4.1E-06	gcm	3.4E+03	water impact
5.7E-06	LAND	2	1.7E-06	gcs	5.4E+03	land impact

Initiator	Water Impact?	#	Frequency (events/yr)	End State	Risk (PF/yr)	Comments
KI10km	Yes	1	2.8E-08	gcs	9.2E+01	water impact
4.0E-08	LAND	2	1.2E-08	gcc	6.8E+01	land impact
					9.3E+04	Total Kinetic Impact Risk

Solar Storm

Initiator	EP outage extent?	#	Frequency (events/yr)	End State	Risk (PF/yr)	Comments
SolStrm	0.25	1	9.3E-04	chaos2	2.3E+04	national EP outage
3.7E-03	0.45	2	1.7E-03	chaos3	2.1E+05	continental EP outage
	0.25	3	9.3E-04	chaos4	4.7E+05	hemispheric EP outage
	0.05	4	1.9E-04	chaos5	3.3E+05	global EP outage
					1.0E+06	Total solar storm risk

Natural Terrestrial Event Trees

Super Volcano events

Initiator	Global cooling?	#	Frequency (events/yr)	End State	Risk (PF/yr)	Comments
SuperV7	No	1	1.4E-05	chaos1	3.4E+01	minimal global coolono - local SLS failure
2.7E-05	moderate (.5)	2	1.4E-05	gcm	1.1E+04	moderate global cooling

Initiator	Global cooling?	#	Frequency (events/yr)	End State	Risk (PF/yr)	Comments
SuperV8	moderate	1	4.1E-06	gcm	3.4E+03	moderate global cooling
8.2E-06	severe (.5)	2	4.1E-06	gcs	1.3E+04	severe global cooling

2.8E+04 Total Volcano Risk

Mega Earthquake

Initiator	Impact in low population area?	#	Frequency (events/yr)	End State	Risk (PF/yr)	Comments
Mquake	Yes	1	9.0E-01	nomega		
9.3E-01	HPZ	2	2.5E-02	equake	6.4E+04	direct fatalities + local SLS failure

Mega Flood

Initiator	Impact in low population area?	#	Frequency (events/yr)	End State	Risk (PF/yr)	Comments
Mflood	GNo	1	3.5E-03	flood	2.0E+04	direct fatalities + local SLS failure

201

Biological Event Trees

Initiator: Natepid (0.04)

Initiator	Med Containment Effective?	SLS Systems Maintained?	#	Frequency (events/yr)	End State	Risk (PF/yr)	Comments
Natepid	Yes	GYes	1	4.19E-02	pand4	4.05E+05	high severity w effective containment
0.04	CFH	Yes	2	8.35E-04	pand5	5.38E+04	high severity w/o effective containment
		SLSP	3	8.35E-04	pand5+	9.69E+04	high severity w/o effective containment + SLS breakdown
				4.36E-02		5.56E+05	Natural pandemic risk

Initiator: bioaccident

Initiator	Med Containment Effective?	SLS systems maintained?	#	Frequency (events/yr)	End State	Risk (PF/yr)	Comments
bioaccident	Yes	GYes	1	4.71E-02	pand4	4.56E+05	high severity w effective containment
	CFH	Yes	2	9.39E-04	pand5	6.06E+04	high severity w/o effective containment
		SLSP	3	9.39E-04	pand5+	1.09E+05	high severity w/o effective containment + SLS breakdown
				4.90E-02		6.25E+05	Total bioaccident risk

Initiator: biolabsab

Initiator	Security measures effective?	Med Containment Effective?	SLS systems maintained?	#	Frequency (events/yr)	End State	Risk (PF/yr)	Comments
biolabsab	Yes	n/a	n/a	1	4.3E-03	nomega		
	SF	Yes	GYes	2	1.2E-03	pand4	1.21E+04	high severity w effective containment
		CFX	Yes	3	2.9E-04	pand5	1.84E+04	high severity w/o effective containment
			SLSP	4	2.9E-04	pand5+	3.32E+04	high severity w/o effective containment + SLS breakdown
					1.8E-03		5.2E+04	Total bio lab sabotage risk

Initiator: bioattack

Initiator	Med Containment Effective?	SLS systems maintained?	#	Frequency (events/yr)	End State	Risk (PF/yr)	Comments
bioattack	Yes	GYes	1	4.2E-04	pand4	4.07E+03	high severity w effective containment
	CFX	Yes	2	1.3E-04	pand5	8.44E+03	high severity w/o effective containment
		SLSP	3	1.3E-04	pand5+	1.52E+04	high severity w/o effective containment + SLS breakdown
				6.8E-04		2.4E+04	Total bio attack risk
						1.26E+06	Total pandemic risk

Terrorism Event Trees

Initiator	Scope of outage limited?	SLS systems maintained?	#	Frequency (events/yr)	End State	Risk (PF/yr)	Comments
epsabotage	Yes	Yes	1	1.59E-03	chaos1	3.99E+03	limited chaos in affected region
		SLSEP	2	6.80E-03	chaos2	1.70E+05	significant chaos in affected region
	EPCW	Yes	3	2.61E-03	chaos2	6.53E+04	limited chaos across continent
		SLSEP	4	2.61E-03	chaos3	3.26E+05	significant chaos across continent
				1.36E-02		3.91E+05	Total EP sabotage risk

Initiator	Low yield weapon?	#	Frequency (events/yr)	End State	Risk (PF/yr)	Comments
nucdet	Yes	1	6.44E-03	nucattack	2.54E+03	low yield weapon
	NWHY	2	3.63E-04	nucattackp	2.39E+02	high yield weapon
			6.80E-03		2.78E+03	Total nuclear terror risk

WAR EVENT TREES

Initiator	Mega Fatality Conflict?	Multi-National War?	Democide?	#	Frequency (events/yr)	End State	Risk (PF/yr)	Comments
armcon	MEGAC	Yes	n/a	1	2.9E-02	iswardths	4.9E+05	Mega fatality interstate war
		CW	DCW	2	2.9E-02	demodths	5.4E+05	Mega fatality civil war + democide
			No	3	4.0E-02	cwdths	4.3E+04	Mega fatality civil war
	No	n/a	GNo	4	3.0E+00	nomega		Low intensity war
					3.08E+00		1.1E+06	Total armed conflict risk

Initiator	<10 warheads launched?	<100 warheads launched?	#	Frequency (events/yr)	End State	Risk (PF/yr)	Comments
lofw	Yes	n/a	1	2.9E-04	swhd10	1643.0564	<10 strategic weapons used
	0.5	Yes	2	1.5E-04	swhd100	1.1E+04	<120 strategic weapons used
		0.5	3	1.5E-04	gcs	4.7E+05	120-1750 strategic weapons used
				5.8E-04		4.9E+05	Total launch on false warning risk

Survival Games

KASHMIR NUCLEAR WAR EVENT TREES

First Strike by	First strike weapons used?	Retaliation weapons used?	Global cooling effects?	#	Frequency (events/yr)	End State	Risk (PF/yr)	Comments
India1	strategic	GYes	GC2	1	1.7E-05	gcm	1.4E+04	<120 strategic weapons used
3.00E-05			No	2	1.30E-05	swhd120	9.9E+02	<120 strategic weapons used
							1.5E+04	India Risk

First Strike by	First strike weapons used?	Retaliation weapons used?	Global cooling effects?	#	Frequency (events/yr)	End State	Risk (PF/yr)	Comments
Pakistan	strategic	GYes	GC2	1	1.7E-04	gcm	1.4E+05	<120 strategic weapons used
3.00E-04			No	2	1.30E-04	swhd120	9.9E+03	<120 strategic weapons used
							1.5E+05	Pakistan Risk
							1.7E+05	Total Kashmir Risk

SIKKIM NUCLEAR WAR EVENT TREES

First Strike by	First strike weapons used?	Retaliation weapons used?	Global cooling effects?	#	Frequency (events/yr)	End State	Risk (PF/yr)	Comments
India2	strategic	GYes	GC2	1	1.70E-05	gcm	1.4E+04	<120 strategic weapons used
1.30E-05			No	2	1.30E-05	swhd120	9.9E+02	<120 strategic weapons used
							1.5E+04	India2

First Strike by	First strike weapons used?	Retaliation weapons used?	Global cooling effects?	#	Frequency (events/yr)	End State	Risk (PF/yr)	Comments
China1	strategic	GYes	GC2	1	1.70E-05	gcm	1.4E+04	<120 strategic weapons used
1.30E-05			No	2	1.30E-05	swhd120	9.9E+02	<120 strategic weapons used
							1.5E+04	China1 Risk
							3.0E+04	Total Sikkim Risk

ISRAEL NUCLEAR WAR EVENT TREES

First Strike by	First strike weapons used?	Retaliation weapons used?	Global cooling effects?	#	Frequency (events/yr)	End State	Risk (PF/yr)	Comments
Israel	strategic	GYes	GC1	1	0.0E+00	gcm	0.0E+00	<50 strategic weapons used
3.00E-05			No	2	3.00E-05	swhd120	2.3E+03	<50 strategic weapons used
							2.3E+03	Israel Risk

First Strike by	First strike weapons used?	Retaliation weapons used?	Global cooling effects?	#	Frequency (events/yr)	End State	Risk (PF/yr)	Comments
Iran	strategic	GYes	GC1	1	0.0E+00	gcm	0.0E+00	<50 strategic weapons used
3.00E-05			No	2	3.00E-05	swhd120	2.3E+03	<50 strategic weapons used
							2.3E+03	Iran Risk
							4.6E+03	Total Israel/Iran Risk

KOREA NUCLEAR WAR EVENT TREES

First Strike by	First strike weapons used?	Retaliation weapons used?	Global cooling effects?	#	Frequency (events/yr)	End State	Risk (PF/yr)	Comments
N Korea 3.00E-03	EMP	tactical (.8)	GNo	1	2.4E-03	twhd100p	3.5E+05	EMP + 100 tactical
		strategic (.1)	GC1	2	0.00E+00	gcm	0.0E+00	<50 strategic weapons used
			No	3	3.00E-04	swhd50+	1.7E+04	50 strategic weapons + EMP
		none (.1)	GNo	4	3.00E-04	chaos2	7.5E+03	EP outage + SLS failure
							3.8E+05	N Korea Risk

First Strike by	First strike weapons used?	Retaliation weapons used?	Global cooling effects?	#	Frequency (events/yr)	End State	Risk (PF/yr)	Comments
USA1 3.00E-03	tactical	tactical (0)	GNo	1	0.0E+00	twhd100	0.0E+00	<100 tactical weapons used
		EMP (.2)	GNo	2	6.00E-04	swhd50+	3.5E+04	50 strategic weapons + EMP
		strategic (.2)	GC1	3	0.00E+00	gcm	0.0E+00	<50 strategic weapons used
			No	4	6.00E-04	swhd50	2.0E+04	<50 strategic weapons used
		none (.6)	GNo	5	1.80E-03	twhd100	1.1E+04	<100 tactical weapons used
							6.5E+04	USA1 Risk
							4.4E+05	Total Korea Risk

SOUTH CHINA SEA NUCLEAR WAR EVENT TREES

First Strike by	First strike weapons used?	Retaliation weapons used?	Global cooling effects?	#	Frequency (events/yr)	End State	Risk (PF/yr)	Comments
China2 3.00E-05	EMP	tactical (.8)	GNo	1	2.4E-05	twhd100p	1.4E+02	EMP + 100 tactical
		strategic (.1)	GYes	2	3.00E-06	gcm	2.5E+03	250-500 strategic weapons used
		none (.1)	GNo	4	3.00E-06	chaos3	3.7E+02	EP outage + SLS failure
							3.0E+03	China2 Risk

First Strike by	First strike weapons used?	Retaliation weapons used?	Global cooling effects?	#	Frequency (events/yr)	End State	Risk (PF/yr)	Comments
USA2 3.00E-04	tactical	tactical (2)	GNo	1	6.0E-05	twhd200	7.0E+02	<200 tactical weapons used
		EMP (.4)	GNo	2	1.20E-04	twhd100p	1.8E+04	tactical + EMP
		strategic (2)	GYes	3	6.00E-05	gcm	5.0E+04	250-500 strategic weapons used
		none (.2)	GNo	4	6.00E-05	twhd100	3.5E+02	<100 tactical weapons used
							6.8E+04	USA2 Risk

7.1E+04   Total S China Sea Risk

UKRAINE NUCLEAR WAR EVENT TREES

First Strike by	First strike weapons used?	Retaliation weapons used?	Global cooling effects?	#	Frequency (events/yr)	End State	Risk (PF/yr)	Comments
Russia1	EMP	tactical (.4)	GNo	1	1.2E-05	twhd100p	1.8E+03	EMP + 100 tactical
3.00E-05		strategic (.1)	GYes	2	3.00E-06	gcc	1.8E+04	>3000 strategic weapons used
		none (.5)	GNo	3	1.50E-05	chaos3	1.9E+03	EP outage + SLS failure
							2.1E+04	Russia1 Risk

First Strike by	First strike weapons used?	Retaliation weapons used?	Global cooling effects?	#	Frequency (events/yr)	End State	Risk (PF/yr)	Comments
USA3	tactical	tactical (.5)	GNo	1	1.5E-04	twhd200	1.7E+03	<200 tactical weapons used
3.00E-04		EMP (.4)	GNo	2	1.20E-04	twhd100p	1.8E+04	tactical + EMP
		strategic (.1)	GYes	3	3.00E-05	gcc	1.8E+05	>3000 strategic weapons used
		none (0)	GNo	4	0.00E+00	twhd100	0.0E+00	<100 tactical weapons used
							1.9E+05	USA3 Risk
							2.2E+05	Total Ukraine Risk

BALTICS/ E EUROPE NUCLEAR WAR EVENT TREES

First Strike by	First strike weapons used?	Retaliation weapons used?	Global cooling effects?	#	Frequency (events/yr)	End State	Risk (PF/yr)	Comments
Russia2	EMP	tactical (.8)	GNo	1	2.4E-05	twhd100p	3.5E+03	EMP + 100 tactical
3.00E-05		strategic (.1)	GYes	2	3.00E-06	gcc	1.8E+04	>3000 strategic weapons used
		none (.1)	GNo	3	3.00E-06	chaos3	3.7E+02	EP outage + SLS failure
							2.1E+04	Russia2 Risk

First Strike by	First strike weapons used?	Retaliation weapons used?	Global cooling effects?	#	Frequency (events/yr)	End State	Risk (PF/yr)	Comments
USA4	tactical	tactical (.5)	GNo	1	1.5E-04	twhd200	1.8E+03	<200 tactical weapons used
3.00E-04		EMP (.4)	GNo	2	1.20E-04	twhd100p	1.8E+04	tactical + EMP
		strategic (.1)	GYes	3	3.00E-05	gcc	1.8E+05	250-500 strategic weapons used
		none (0)	GNo	4	0.00E+00	twhd100	0.0E+00	<100 tactical weapons used
							1.9E+05	USA4 Risk
							2.2E+05	Total Baltics/ E Europe Risk

SYRIA/IRAQ NUCLEAR WAR EVENT TREES

First Strike by	First strike weapons used?	Retaliation weapons used?	Global cooling effects?	#	Frequency (events/yr)	End State	Risk (PF/yr)	Comments
Russia3	EMP	tactical (.8)	GNo	1	2.4E-04	twhd100p	3.5E+04	EMP + 100 tactical
3.00E-04		strategic (.1)	GYes	2	3.00E-05	gcc	1.8E+05	>3000 strategic weapons used
		none (.1)	GNo	3	3.00E-05	chaos3	3.7E+03	EP outage + SLS failure
							2.1E+05	Russia3 Risk

First Strike by	First strike weapons used?	Retaliation weapons used?	Global cooling effects?	#	Frequency (events/yr)	End State	Risk (PF/yr)	Comments
USA5	tactical	tactical (.5)	GNo	1	1.5E-03	twhd200	1.8E+04	<200 tactical weapons used
3.00E-03		EMP (.4)	GNo	2	1.20E-03	twhd100p	1.8E+05	tactical + EMP
		strategic (.1)	GYes	3	3.00E-04	gcc	1.8E+06	250-500 strategic weapons used
		none (0)	GNo	4	0.00E+00	twhd100	0.0E+00	<100 tactical weapons used
							1.9E+06	USA5 Risk
							2.2E+06	Total Syria/Iraq Risk

CRASHWAR NUCLEAR WAR EVENT TREES

First Strike by	First strike weapons used?	Retaliation weapons used?	Global cooling effects?	#	Frequency (events/yr)	End State	Risk (PF/yr)	Comments
China3 3.00E-04	EMP	tactical (.8)	GNo	1	2.4E-04	twhd100p	1.4E+03	EMP + 100 tactical
		strategic (.1)	GYes	2	3.00E-05	gcm	2.5E+04	250-500 strategic weapons used
		none (.1)	GNo	4	3.00E-05	chaos3	3.7E+03	EP outage + SLS failure
							3.0E+04	China3 Risk

First Strike by	First strike weapons used?	Retaliation weapons used?	Global cooling effects?	#	Frequency (events/yr)	End State	Risk (PF/yr)	Comments
USA6 3.00E-03	tactical	tactical (.2)	GNo	1	6.0E-04	twhd200	7.0E+03	<200 tactical weapons used
		EMP (.4)	GNo	2	1.20E-03	twhd100p	1.8E+05	tactical + EMP
		strategic (.2)	GYes	3	6.00E-04	gcm	5.0E+05	250-500 strategic weapons used
		none (.2)	GNo	4	6.00E-04	twhd100	3.5E+03	<100 tactical weapons used
							6.8E+05	USA6 Risk
							7.1E+05	Total Crashwar Risk

Survival Games

MEGA FATALITY RISK ASSESSMENT RESULTS

#	Initiator	Scenario #	Frequency (events/yr)	End State	Risk (PF/yr)	Risk Rank (%)
1	KI10m	KI10m	3.4E-03	PF10m	4.1E+03	0.0%
2	KI100m	KI100m1	2.3E-04	pf100m	3.7E+03	0.0%
3	KI100m	KI100m2	9.2E-05	gcm	7.6E+04	0.9%
4	KI1km	KI1km1	4.1E-06	gcm	3.4E+03	0.0%
5	KI1km	KI1km2	1.7E-06	gcs	5.4E+03	0.1%
6	KI10km	KI10km1	2.8E-08	gcs	9.2E+01	0.0%
7	KI10km	KI10km2	1.2E-08	gcc	6.8E+01	0.0%
8	SuperV	SuperV71	1.4E-05	chaos1	3.4E+01	0.0%
9	SuperV	SuperV72	1.4E-05	gcm	1.1E+04	0.1%
10	SuperV	SuperV81	4.1E-06	gcm	3.4E+03	0.0%
11	SuperV	SuperV82	4.1E-06	gcs	1.3E+04	0.2%
12	Mquake	Mquake	2.5E-02	equake	6.4E+04	0.7%
13	Mflood	Mflood	3.5E-03	flood	2.0E+04	0.2%
14	SolStrm	SolStrm1	9.3E-04	chaos2	2.3E+04	0.3%
15	SolStrm	SolStrm2	1.7E-03	chaos3	2.1E+05	2.4%
16	SolStrm	SolStrm3	9.3E-04	chaos4	4.7E+05	5.4%
17	SolStrm	SolStrm4	1.9E-04	chaos5	3.3E+05	3.8%
18	Natepid	Natepid1	4.2E-02	pand4	4.1E+05	4.7%
19	Natepid	Natepid2	8.4E-04	pand5	5.4E+04	0.6%
20	Natepid	Natepid3	8.3E-04	pand5+	9.7E+04	1.1%
21	bioaccident	bioaccident1	4.7E-02	pand4	4.6E+05	5.3%
22	bioaccident	bioaccident2	9.39E-04	pand5	6.1E+04	0.7%
23	bioaccident	bioaccident3	9.39E-04	pand5+	1.1E+05	1.3%
24	biolabsab	biolabsab2	1.2E-03	pand4	1.2E+04	0.1%
25	biolabsab	biolabsab3	2.9E-04	pand5	1.8E+04	0.2%
26	biolabsab	biolabsab4	2.9E-04	pand5+	3.3E+04	0.4%
27	bioattack	bioattack1	4.2E-04	pand4	4.1E+03	0.0%
28	bioattack	bioattack2	1.3E-04	pand5	8.4E+03	0.1%
29	bioattack	bioattack3	1.3E-04	pand5+	1.5E+04	0.2%
30	epsabotage	epsabotage1	1.6E-03	chaos1	4.0E+03	0.0%
31	epsabotage	epsabotage2	6.8E-03	chaos2	1.7E+05	2.0%
32	epsabotage	epsabotage3	2.61E-03	chaos2	6.5E+04	0.8%
33	epsabotage	epsabotage4	2.61E-03	chaos3	3.3E+05	3.8%
34	nucdet	nucdet1	6.44E-03	nucattack	2.5E+03	0.0%
35	nucdet	nucdet2	3.63E-04	nucattackp	2.4E+02	0.0%
36	armcon	armcon1	2.9E-02	iswardths	4.9E+05	5.7%
37	armcon	armcon2	2.9E-02	demodths	5.4E+05	6.2%
38	armcon	armcon3	4.0E-02	cwdths	4.3E+04	0.5%
39	lofw	lofw1	2.9E-04	swhd10	1.6E+03	0.0%
40	lofw	lofw2	1.5E-04	swhd100	1.1E+04	0.1%
41	lofw	lofw3	1.5E-04	gcs	4.7E+05	5.5%
42	Kashmir	India11	1.7E-05	gcm	1.4E+04	0.2%
43	Kashmir	India12	1.30E-05	swhd120	9.9E+02	0.0%
44	Kashmir	Pakistan1	1.7E-04	gcm	1.4E+05	1.6%
45	Kashmir	Pakistan2	1.3E-04	swhd120	9.9E+03	0.1%
46	Sikkim	India21	1.7E-05	gcm	1.4E+04	0.2%
47	Sikkim	India22	1.3E-05	swhd120	9.9E+02	0.0%
48	Sikkim	China11	1.7E-05	gcm	1.4E+04	0.2%
49	Sikkim	China12	1.3E-05	swhd120	9.9E+02	0.0%

Survival Games

MEGA FATALITY RISK ASSESSMENT RESULTS

#	Initiator	Scenario #	Frequency (events/yr)	End State	Risk (PF/yr)	Risk Rank (%)
50	Israel	Israel1	0.0E+00	gcm	0.0E+00	0.0%
51	Israel	Israel2	3.0E-05	swhd120	2.3E+03	0.0%
52	Israel	Iran1	0.0E+00	gcm	0.0E+00	0.0%
53	Israel	Iran2	3.0E-05	swhd120	2.3E+03	0.0%
54	Korea	NKorea1	2.4E-03	twhd100p	3.5E+05	4.0%
55	Korea	NKorea2	0.0E+00	gcm	0.0E+00	0.0%
56	Korea	NKorea3	3.0E-04	swhd50+	1.7E+04	0.2%
57	Korea	NKorea4	3.0E-04	chaos2	7.5E+03	0.1%
58	Korea	USAone1	0.0E+00	gcm	0.0E+00	0.0%
59	Korea	USAone2	6.0E-04	swhd50+	3.5E+04	0.4%
60	Korea	USAone3	0.0E+00	gcm	0.0E+00	0.0%
61	Korea	USAone4	6.0E-04	swhd50	2.0E+04	0.2%
62	Korea	USAone5	1.8E-03	twhd100	1.1E+04	0.1%
63	S China Sea	China21	2.4E-05	twhd100p	1.4E+02	0.0%
64	S China Sea	China22	3.0E-06	gcm	2.5E+03	0.0%
65	S China Sea	China23	3.0E-06	chaos3	3.7E+02	0.0%
66	S China Sea	USAtwo1	6.0E-05	twhd200	7.0E+02	0.0%
67	S China Sea	USAtwo2	1.2E-04	twhd100p	1.8E+04	0.2%
68	S China Sea	USAtwo3	6.0E-05	gcm	5.0E+04	0.6%
69	S China Sea	USAtwo4	6.0E-05	twhd100	3.5E+02	0.0%
70	Ukraine	Russia11	1.2E-05	twhd100p	1.8E+03	0.0%
71	Ukraine	Russia12	3.0E-06	gcc	1.8E+04	0.2%
72	Ukraine	Russia13	1.5E-05	chaos3	1.9E+03	0.0%
73	Ukraine	USAthree1	1.5E-04	twhd200	1.7E+03	0.0%
74	Ukraine	USAthree2	1.2E-04	twhd100p	1.8E+04	0.2%
75	Ukraine	USAthree3	3.0E-05	gcc	1.8E+05	2.0%
76	Ukraine	USAthree4	0.0E+00	twhd100	0.0E+00	0.0%
77	E Europe	Russia21	2.4E-05	twhd100p	3.5E+03	0.0%
78	E Europe	Russia22	3.0E-06	gcc	1.8E+04	0.2%
79	E Europe	Russia23	3.0E-06	chaos3	3.7E+02	0.0%
80	E Europe	USAfour1	1.5E-04	twhd200	1.8E+03	0.0%
81	E Europe	USAfour2	1.2E-04	twhd100p	1.8E+04	0.2%
82	E Europe	USAfour3	3.0E-05	gcc	1.8E+05	2.0%
83	E Europe	USAfour4	0.0E+00	twhd100	0.0E+00	0.0%
84	Syria/Iraq	Russia31	2.4E-04	twhd100p	3.5E+04	0.4%
85	Syria/Iraq	Russia32	3.0E-05	gcc	1.8E+05	2.0%
86	Syria/Iraq	Russia33	3.0E-05	chaos3	3.7E+03	0.0%
87	Syria/Iraq	USAfive1	1.5E-03	twhd200	1.8E+04	0.2%
88	Syria/Iraq	USAfive2	1.2E-03	twhd100p	1.8E+05	2.0%
89	Syria/Iraq	USAfive3	3.0E-04	gcc	1.8E+06	20.3%
90	Syria/Iraq	USAfive4	0.0E+00	twhd100	0.0E+00	0.0%
91	Crashwar	China31	2.4E-04	twhd100p	1.4E+03	0.0%
92	Crashwar	China32	3.0E-05	gcm	2.5E+04	0.3%
93	Crashwar	China33	3.0E-05	chaos3	3.7E+03	0.0%
94	Crashwar	USAsix1	6.0E-04	twhd200	7.0E+03	0.1%
95	Crashwar	USAsix2	1.2E-03	twhd100p	1.8E+05	2.0%
96	Crashwar	USAsix3	6.0E-04	gcm	5.0E+05	5.7%
97	Crashwar	USAsix4	6.0E-04	twhd100	3.5E+03	0.0%

Total Mega Fatality Risk **8.65E+06** 100.0%

Total Individual Mega Fatality Risk 1.20E-03

Model References

The following references are called out in the MFRA risk model, or provide good background for the following subjects.

Kinetic Impact Events
1. Impact Event, *Wikipedia*, 7/20/2014
2. Population Agglomerations of the World, Thomas Brinkhoff: City Population, *http://www.citypopulation.de*
3. Medium-Size Asteroid Strike Could Unleash a Mini Ice Age, Mike Wall, Space.com, 2/9/2016
4. Asteroid impact effects and their immediate hazards for human populations, Rumpf, et al, Geophysical Research Letters, March 2017
5. A probabilistic asteroid impact risk model: assessment of sub-300 m impacts, Mathias, et al, NASA Ames Research Center, February 2017

Natural Terrestrial Events
10. *Global Volcanic Hazards and Risk*, Loughlin, et al, Cambridge University Press, 2015
11. Supervolcano, *Wikipedia*, 7/20/2014
12. Volcano Hazards Program, U.S. Geological Survey, http://volcanoes.usgs.gov/
13. Earthquake Hazards Program, U.S. Geological Survey, http://earthquake.usgs.gov/
14. List of Deadliest Floods, *Wikipedia*, 7/20/2014
15. List of Famines, *Wikipedia*, 9/4/2014
16. Magnetic Pole Reversal Happens All The (Geologic) Time, NASA.gov

Electric Power Failure Risks
20. Large Power Transformers and the U.S. Electric Grid, U.S. Department of Energy, 2012
Solar Storms
21. Solar Storm Threat Analysis, James A. Marusek, *Impact* 2007
22. eXtreme Space Weather Events: Probabilities and Uncertainties, Pete Riley, Predictive Science Inc. 4/5/2016
23. Solar Storm Risk to the North American Electric Grid, Lloyd's 2013

24. Near Miss: The Solar Superstorm of July 2012, Phillips, Tony, *NASA Science News*, 7/23/2013
25. Severe Space Weather--Social and Economic Impacts, Phillips, Tony, *NASA Science News*, 1/21/2009
26. Severe Space Weather Events—Understanding Societal and Economic Impacts Workshop Report, National Research Council, 2008

EMP
30. Report of the Commission to Assess the Threat to the United States from Electromagnetic Pulse (EMP) Attack, Graham, et al, 2004
31. Report of the Commission to Assess the Threat to the United States from Electromagnetic Pulse (EMP) Attack, Graham, et al, 2008
32. "Electromagnetic Pulse: Threat to Critical Infrastructure", Dr. Peter Vincent Pry Testimony Before The Subcommittee on Cybersecurity, Infrastructure Protection and Security Technologies, House Committee on Homeland Security, 5/8/2014
33. Testimony of Dr. Michael J. Frankel to the House Homeland Security Committee Hearing Sub-Committee On Cyber Security, Infrastructure Protection, And Security Technologies, May 8, 2014
34. Failure to Protect U.S. Against Electromagnetic Pulse Threat Could Make 9/11 Look Trivial Someday, Kelly-Detwiler, Peter, *Forbes*, 7/31/2014
35. The Growing Threat From an EMP Attack, R. James Woolsey & Peter Vincent Pry, *The Wall Street Journal*, 8/13/2014

Electric Power Sabotage
40. Assault on California Power Station Raises Alarm on Potential for Terrorism, Rebecca Smith, *The Wall Street Journal*, 2/5/2014
41. America's Power Is Under Threat, Peggy Noonan, *The Wall Street Journal*, 2/7/2014
42. U.S. Risks National Blackout From Small-Scale Attack, Rebecca Smith, *The Wall Street Journal*, 3/12/2014

43. DOE: Information on Power Grid Threats Should Have Been Classified, Rebecca Smith, *The Wall Street Journal*, 4/9/2014
44. Federal Government Is Urged to Prevent Grid Attacks, Rebecca Smith, *The Wall Street Journal*, 7/7/2014
45. Power Station's Security Is Breached, Again, Rebecca Smith, *The Wall Street Journal*, 8/29/2014

Pandemic Risks
50. List of epidemics, *Wikipedia*, 7/20/2014
51. BSL-4 Laboratories as of 2010-2011, Federation of American Scientists
52. How secure are labs handling world's deadliest pathogens?, Sharon Begley and Julie Steenhuysen, *Reuters*, 2/15/2012
53. Pandemic Severity Index, Centers for Disease Control and Prevention, http://www.cdc.gov/media/pdf/MitigationSlides.pdf
54. Influenza Pandemic Periodicity, Virus Recycling, and the Art of Risk Assessment, Walter R. Dowdle, *Emerging Infectious Diseases*, Vol. 12, No. 1, January 2006
55. Ebola's Warning for an Unprepared America, *The Wall Street Journal*, 9/17/2014
56. Day of synthetic pathogens-based bioterrorism nears, *Homeland Security Newsletter*, 9/16/2010
57. Experiments with dangerous bird flu stains pose risk of accidental release, *Homeland Security Newsletter*, 5/27/2014
58. Nearly 400 Accidents with Dangerous Pathogens and Biotoxins Reported in U.S. Labs over 7 Years, Katherine Harmon Courage, *Scientific American*, 10/3/2011
59. CDC scientist took shortcuts handling deadly bird flu virus, investigation finds, Lena H. Sun and Brady Dennis, *The Washington Post*, 8/15/2014
60. More deadly pathogens, toxins found improperly stored in NIH and FDA labs, Lena H. Sun and Brady Dennis, *The Washington Post*, 9/5/2014
61. Ebola is 'devouring everything in its path.' Could it lead to Liberia's collapse?, Abby Ohlheiser, *The Washington Post*, 9/12/2014

62. Anthrax Scare at CDC Labs, Betsy McKay, *The Wall Street Journal*, 6/20/2014

63. Accidents Prompt CDC to Halt Lab Sample Shipments, *The Wall Street Journal*, 7/12/2014

64. CDC Lab Head resigns After Anthrax Incident, *The Wall Street Journal*, 7/24/2014

65. *The Demon in the Freezer*, Richard Preston, Random House, 2012

War

70. U.S. and Russian Launch-Ready Nuclear Weapons: A Threat to All Nations and Peoples, Steven Starr, Senior Scientist, PSR

71. List of wars 1945–1989, *Wikipedia*, 7/16/2014

72. List of wars 1990–2002, *Wikipedia*, 7/16/2014

73. *The Better Angels of Our Nature*, Steven Pinker, Viking Penguin, 2011

74. Power Failure, Robert Kagan, *The Wall Street Journal*, 9/6/2014

75. In Fight for Syria, Food and Medicine Are Weapons of War, *The Wall Street Journal*, 1/21/2014

76. Asian Nations Fear War with China, *The Wall Street Journal*, 7/15/2014

77. The Growing Threat From an EMP Attack, R. James Woolsey & Peter Vincent Pry, *The Wall Street Journal*, 8/13/2014

78. *The World America Made*, Robert Kagan, Alfred A. Knopf, 2012, ISBN 978-0-307-96131-0

General Risk Analysis References

100. *Risk Management Revisited*, JP Kindinger, Kindinger Strategic Advisors, 2015.

101. On the Quantitative Definition of Risk, Stanley Kaplan & B John Garrick, *Risk Analysis*, 1981.

102. *Reactor Safety Study, An Assessment of Accident Risks in*

103. *U.S. Commercial Nuclear Power Plants*, U.S. Nuclear Regulatory Commission, October 1975.

104. *Fault Tree Handbook with Aerospace Applications*, NASA Office of Safety and Mission Assurance, August, 2002.

105. The Beginning of the Monte Carlo Method, N. Metropolis, *Los Alamos Science*, 1987.
106. On the Estimation of Binomial Success Probability with Zero Occurrence in Sample, Mehdi Razzaghi, *Journal of Modern Applied Statistical Methods*, November 2002.
107. Estimating the Probability of Rare Events: Addressing Zero Failure Data, John Quigley & Mathew Revie, *Risk Analysis*, July 2011.

Appendix C - Risk Management Glossary

Aleatory uncertainty.- Aleatory uncertainty is the inherent randomness that remains after all relevant and available knowledge about an event or condition has been discovered.

Conditional probability – The likelihood that an event in a scenario occurs, or not, conditioned on all the events that precede it in the scenario.

Consequence analysis – Assesses the resulting damage or loss that would be realized for each scenario, given that it occurs. The results of the risk analysis are then obtained by summing all the conditional damages by the frequencies of the corresponding scenarios.

Consequence measures – Metrics defined to measure injury or loss incurred from a risk scenario. Examples include human deaths and monetary loss.

Continuous distribution – A probability distribution where a random variable can take on any value between the specified low and high limits.

Defense in depth – A risk management strategy that employs redundant and diverse risk reduction actions to address hazards.

Discrete distribution – A probability distribution where the variable under study can only take on certain specific values (e.g. heads or tails).

Dynamic simulation – A mathematical modeling tool that predicts the behavior of a defined system as a function of time.

Epistemic uncertainty - Epistemic uncertainty is the uncertainty arising from imperfect knowledge about the event or condition in question.

Event tree – An inductive logic modeling tool that charts the progression of a scenario from an initiating event through conditional top events to an end state.

Event tree end state – A stable condition realized at the conclusion of a risk scenario.

Event tree initiating event – The first event in a scenario.

Event tree scenario – A predicted series of events leading from an initiating event to a measurable end state. A risk analysis includes a description of the "as planned" scenario which generally defines success for the planned endeavor as well as failure scenarios which end in various degrees of injury, loss, or damage.

Event tree split fraction – The conditional probability assigned to a branch point in an event tree.

Event tree top event – Questions listed on the top of an event tree that describe conditional events that may or may not occur to define a scenario.

Fault tree – A deductive logic modeling tool that illustrates the logical paths from elementary basic events to a specified top event.

Frequency – The quantitative result of an experiment involving repeated trials. Frequency can be expressed as the number of events observed in a measured number of trials (N/T) or as the number of events observed per unit of time (e.g. deaths per year).

Hazard – An inherent physical characteristic that has the potential for causing harm to people, property, or the environment.

Likelihood – The chance that something will happen

Likelihood analysis – Determines the resulting frequency of each possible scenario from the Scenario Analysis. The sum of all the scenario frequencies must equal the initiating event frequency.

Master logic diagram - A deductive logic modeling tool that illustrates all possible logical paths through which scenarios must pass to produce a specified top event.

Monte Carlo simulation – A calculation performed repeatedly with parameter values selected randomly from probability distributions.

Probability – The science of determining likelihood from limited or no frequency type data. Probability is the numerical expression of a state of knowledge or confidence.

Qualitative risk assessment – A risk analysis performed using methods that rank the likelihood and consequence of risk scenarios in a relative sense: that is relative to each other (more, about the same, less) and/or a qualitative ranking scale (e.g. high, medium, low).

Quantitative risk assessment – A risk analysis performed using methods that express the likelihood and consequences of risk scenarios on absolute numeric scales.

Risk – The chance of injury, loss, or damage resulting from exposure to a hazard. Expressed symbolically, Risk = Hazard/Safeguards. Risk can also be thought of as uncertainty that matters. An example of the difference between risk and uncertainty is illustrated by an inheritance of an unknown amount. The recipient of the inheritance may have great uncertainty about how much he or she will receive, but there is no risk.

Risk assessment/analysis – The science of predicting future conditions considering the possible success or failure of planned actions in the presence of hazards.

Risk curve – A graphic plot describing the assessed range of possible frequency and consequence results for a risk scenario or category of scenarios.

Risk management – The science of using risk analysis to make informed decisions with imperfect knowledge.

Risk matrix – A graphic arrangement of rows and columns where categories of likelihood and consequence are used to rank potential risk events or issues.

Risk watch list – A ranked list of assessed risk issues complete with recommended risk reduction actions.

Safeguards – Protective or mitigative measures reducing the chance of injury, loss, or damage resulting from exposure to a hazard

Statistics – The science of determining likelihood from available frequency type data

System - An entity comprised of interacting discrete elements functioning to achieve some beneficial objective.

Uncertainty analysis – An assessment of the confidence with which the likelihood analysis and consequence analysis questions can be answered, this is expressed in terms of probability.

Acknowledgements

Doing nerdy analytical work in my spare time comes naturally to me, but organizing it into something comprehensive is definitely work and I've had a lot help in producing *Survival Games*. The biggest contribution, of course, comes from the patience shown by my wife Cindy Kindinger for all the time spent on this project. The quality of *Survival Games* also was vastly improved by the thorough review of the rough draft performed by my dear friend and Triangle Fraternity Brother Dr. J. Frank Sherwood. Finally, a special thanks goes to Glendon Haddix at Streetlight Graphics who turned my vague idea for a cover into something truly special.

JP Kindinger, 9/25/2017

Index

About the Author

John P. Kindinger is an author and semi-retired engineer living in Eustis, Florida. Before moving to Florida, John was employed at the Los Alamos National Laboratory where he served as Nuclear Design and Risk Analysis Group Leader. Prior to joining LANL, John was Manager of Risk Assessment Technology at ARES Corporation and a senior consultant with Pickard, Lowe, & Garrick (PLG), Inc. in Newport Beach, CA. Before that, he was employed as a staff engineer for the Consumers Power Company in Jackson, Michigan.

John has extensive experience in the assessment of risk for complex projects and important investment decisions and safety analysis for defense nuclear facilities, nuclear power plants, and other high hazard facilities. He holds a BS in Mechanical Engineering from Michigan State University and a MS in the Management of Technology from the Massachusetts Institute of Technology.

Follow John's activities at jpkindinger.com.

www.ingramcontent.com/pod-product-compliance
Lightning Source LLC
Chambersburg PA
CBHW060843280326
41934CB00007B/897